"When it comes to crisis response and safeguarding your company's reputation, Molly is one of the best in the world. Her advice is on point, her instincts are impeccable, and her ability to execute is masterful. Molly isn't one of those 'theoretical' crisis experts. Her expertise was earned the hard way . . . by slogging it out in the trenches in real-life crisis situations. If you're responsible in any way for your company's reputation, you need to put this book at the top of your reading list."

—Warren Weeks, Principal, Weeks Media

"I have dealt with a crisis or two and maybe even caused a few on my own, so I appreciate Molly McPherson's insights from *Indestructible: Reclaim Control and Respond with Confidence in a Media Crisis.* Every organization, business, or political candidate will face some sort of crisis. Her thoughts on not only how to deal with them but then actually get a handle on all aspects of public affairs, especially in getting comfortable with using social media in a crisis, is invaluable."

—Rear Admiral ADM (Ret.) Timothy Sullivan, USCG

"Molly McPherson is the only person I know in reputation management who truly understands how to harness the power and potential of social media. She can show you how to make it work for you, rather than against you."

—Jeanne Meserve, Emmy Award-Winning Anchor
and Correspondent, CNN and ABC News

"Molly McPherson is a communications first responder! Crisis management, social media strategy, brand enhancement. I have her on speed dial. So should you."

—Jeffrey Blount, Author of *The Emancipation of Evan Walls*,
Former Senior Director, NBC News Washington

"For years, Molly McPherson has stood out as one of the savviest media and crisis communicators working today. Her work goes far beyond the usual platitudes to deal with the hard-nosed realities of individuals and brands in trouble—whether caused by actual bad acts or the mere *perception* of bad acts. In *Indestructible: Reclaim Control and Respond with Confidence in a Media Crisis,* she shares clear-eyed thinking that communicators and others in the spotlight should internalize *before* trouble comes knocking on their front door—or their Twitter feed."

—Brad Phillips, President, Throughline Group,
and Author of *The Media Training Bible*

"For PR professionals, the words 'cancel culture' mean more than just a person, group, or company paying the ultimate price for a mistake; they also flag failures to communicate.

"Not only does Molly provide you with the preparations to make before 'cancel culture' comes calling, but the paths to take when the pressure is on so you'll avoid adding to the anger. With this book in your back pocket, you can be confident in knowing you'll be indestructible during a crisis."

—Mike McGill, President, WaterPIO,
and Former Producer, CNN's Reliable Sources

"Throughout Molly's career she's done a great job of moving forward the conversation with sharp insights around media relations during a crisis. *Indestructible* will go a long way continuing her great advice for communicators and the companies they serve."

—Bill Coletti, Author of *Critical Moments:
The New Mindset of Reputation Management*

INDESTRUCTIBLE

INDESTRUCTIBLE

RECLAIM CONTROL AND RESPOND WITH CONFIDENCE IN A MEDIA CRISIS

MOLLY McPHERSON

Published by Mandala Tree Press
mandalatreepress.com

Paperback ISBN: 978-1-954801-08-0
Hardback ISBN: 978-1-954801-10-3
Ebook ISBN: 978-1-954801-09-7

BUS071000 BUSINESS & ECONOMICS / Leadership
BUS052000 BUSINESS & ECONOMICS / Public Relations

Cover design © 2021 Molly McPherson
Cover designed by Angela Baxter
Edited by Deborah Spencer
Typeset by Kaitlin Barwick

mollymcpherson.com

For Rory, who makes hard work look easy. I salute you.

To Kathleen, who will prove that people who
grow up in-between always come out ahead.

To Conor, who appreciates entrepreneurship, social media,
and what makes Fenway so special in April.

And to Quinn, whose smile is like a "For You" page.
It's the first thing we always see.

CONTENTS

PREFACE

The idea for this book began with a simple set of questions:

- What characteristics and behaviors of leaders and public figures harm their reputations in the digital age?
- How do some leaders navigate the treacherous digital landscape while others drown due to it?
- Where are the communicators? Is anyone listening to them? Do they even have a seat at the table?

The practice of public relations has always involved taking measures to protect reputations against various potential dangers. But in the digital age, the speed and spread of communications mean the older tools are no longer effective. It's not solely that public sentiment sways against an organization or individual and gradually erodes their reputation—it's beyond that now. The anger and misgivings caused by reports of unacceptable behavior lead to a near-instantaneous and almost irrefutable presumption of guilt. The consequences of such a conclusion are summarized in a phrase: "cancel culture."

My first inkling that there could be a volatile connection between news and viral social media stemmed from a news story that exploded online in July 2015. The story involved a Minnesotan on a big game hunt in Zimbabwe and a thirteen-year-old lion. However, that wasn't the headline that drew enough attention to go viral.

The lion had a name and was an iconic fixture at the Hwange National Park in western Zimbabwe.

The big game hunter also had a name, but one that wouldn't raise much recognition from people outside of family, friends, professional colleagues, and patients.

But that all changed . . . quickly.

The British media was the first to take notice of the story that quickly picked up steam online, and a viral news story was born from the death of Cecil.

The big game hunter now had a name and a profession to add color to the story; Dr. Walter Palmer from Eden Prairie, Minnesota, was now the hunted.

The press descended on Palmer's dental practice and his home. Across the globe, people excoriated Palmer for his role in the death of Cecil the Lion (in death, now even more beloved).

Actress Mia Farrow, who knows a thing or two about being at the center of a media firestorm, tweeted the address of Dr. Palmer. The since-deleted tweet was a shot to the heart of Palmer's reputation.

"#CecilTheLion-Gentle protector of 6 cubs. Loved by many. Killed by Dentist Walter Palmer," Farrow tweeted Wednesday, followed by Palmer's address.

From the famous to the conservationists, Palmer was the target of a mob of angry online vigilantes who wanted him to suffer. Not unlike the suffering Cecil experienced in his last day of life.

After I wrote a blog post about the swift online rebuke of Dr. Palmer, I was asked to speak as a guest on the *Knowledge@Wharton* radio program on Sirius XM. I remarked in the interview that the story spun so wildly out of Dr. Palmer's control due to his actions that had little to do with the death of Cecil—actions of earlier big game hunts.

Photos from hunts of Palmer and his friends posing behind their previous kills likely triggered someone on Palmer's Facebook page to take notice. I have no way of knowing if there was a mole in Palmer's Facebook friends list, but my experience in online reputational management tells me that one photo in particular was the portent of reputational death.

That photo is difficult to look at in the context of the details of Cecil's death. Palmer is kneeling behind a lion with its eyes closed and a gash on its head—presumably dead. There is a bow leaning on the lion's head just below another man who is grinning ear-to-ear like Palmer. The photo posted on Palmer's Facebook page was not of Cecil, but of another lion.

But that didn't matter.

The image of Dr. Palmer and his fellow big game hunter posing over a dead lion was proof to many that he was a monster for killing Cecil. Images or video are the visual accelerant to any viral story. Here we had a photo of a dentist—who is known to pay hefty prices for access to big game kill opportunities—with a dead lion. The optics (the story gleaned from a visual of a dead lion) killed Palmer's reputation.

The online outrage was swift and fierce. So was the scene at his practice, where protestors—many armed with stuffed lions—demonstrated in front of his office. The mix of online and in-person, offline vitriol sparked a movement against the dentist.

Here we are, now over five years later, and Dr. Palmer is no longer a trending news story, but thanks to archival news stories and social media posts, the story will live on forever and the reputational damage to Palmer will last a lifetime as well.

THE PUBLIC BITES BACK

Judging by critical comments about his dental practice posted on the review site Yelp, Google reviews, and the comment section on news stories (not to mention the scathing social media posts), the reputational damage was devastating to him personally and professionally.

As the Palmer story unfolded, I knew with certainty the culprit behind the velocity of the story was social media. The reason everyone seemed to learn of the name Dr. Walter Palmer, seemingly overnight, was due to social media. I was convinced then that all my future work—workshops, podcasts, public relations advice—would be shaped by the influence of this relatively new medium.

The idea that social media is altering crisis communications and reputation management is now a reality.

No longer is it the news media alone that could make or break a person's or a brand's reputation—social media will likely always play a role now. Social media is as powerful as a major news outlet when it comes to framing a reputation. One social media post, no matter where it originates, can enhance a reputation or trash it if it goes viral.

As a public relations practitioner who has helped leaders and communicators navigate message response in the digital age for over twenty-five years, I have had a front row seat to this online warfare. I have written plenty of crisis toolkits and have counseled many leaders who are struggling to understand how to manage their customers' expectations in an age when it only takes one negative tweet or hashtag to send an organization into a death spiral. I am often the one who alerts them to the social media rebellions happening through a Facebook group or hashtag campaign. Or they come to me after learning about a digital revolt led by some of their customers or by activist groups.

These leaders usually need insight in two areas:

1. The actual level of fury
2. What it will take to make it go away

There is a predictability to a negative turn on trending social media that I can usually spot in the early stages. I find it fairly easy to finger the names of people who will survive a full-blown crisis as well as the ones who are doomed right out the gate. Every day, organizations, business leaders, celebrities, and other public figures land on the wrong side of public opinion.

I make a point of noticing.

WHAT'S THE SCOOP?

I have always had a nose for news and a sense that social media, when first introduced to the mainstream, was going to be a game changer, not only for communications but for crisis management. Mix that nose for news with a keen awareness of the moment when risky behaviors or decisions collide with defective communications, and you have me in a nutshell.

I live for this stuff. My fascination with following crash-and-burn PR stories in the news is only matched by my desire to help clients prevent it from happening in the first place. If you find yourself in a reputational spin because your communications or business methods are out of step with the online hoi polloi, then I'm your gal. I help people, many of them leaders, become indestructible in the modern age of digital media.

As it so happens, Dr. Palmer resides in the state where I was born and raised, Minnesota. And it also so happens, he lives near one of my long-time friends, who kept me up to date on what was happening at the dental practice and as well as the home of her infamous neighbor. She reported a lot of handmade signs and lions. Lots of stuffed lions. My friend offered to stop by his house and recommend my services to help him handle the local and international groundswell of negative publicity.

I thanked her for thinking of me, but I was much happier discussing the story of the "dentist and the lion" from where I was, rather than working it from the inside. As a sidenote, the crisis manager who helped Palmer craft his initial statement distanced himself only later. On Twitter, crisis manager Jon Austin posted, "Yesterday another PR firm asked (sic) to help distribute Dr. Palmer's statement. Having completed that task, we've ended our work on this issue."

POP GOES YOUR EGO

It's not always easy to be the person who tells it like it is. People don't like that person.

I'm a truth-teller. Every personality quiz I've taken tells me that's what I am wired to do. I call it as I see it. I carry and use the yardstick that measures the public's sentiment, then I tell my clients what I've found.

Many times, I feel like a pin invited to a balloon party. I'm the one who pops egos, blows up current communication plans and resources, and offers a message not well received by many organizational leaders.

I don't often speak from my opinion alone; I speak from my experience as a PR advisor, a woman, a consumer, and a mother to four teen-agers. I am also a proud Gen Xer from the Midwest, who grew up as a middle child in one of the Twin Cities. You don't get any more middle-of-the-road than that.

I can clearly see both sides of a controversy but can identify the side the public will fall on. If there are different pathways to take out of a PR mess, I point out the safer one to take. If I spot risks, I tell you. If it hurts, then you'll know I'm close to the truth.

When I run into opposition, it's because someone has judged me rather than evaluating the situation. The person who fights with me the most is usually the person who is the cause or the gateway to the problem.

I know which type of person is more likely to speak up and why. I know how old they are and what their comfort level is with technology and sharing their lives online, specifically with social media.

I read textbooks and newly released studies on public opinion, media, and public relations to help shape my advice to my clients, customers, and podcast listeners. As I age, I am less inclined to rely on opinion; however, I will admit to following up on my gut reactions to see if it checks with my advice. That's not simply talk—I am not someone who relies on opinion. Perhaps it's my midwestern upbringing or being a middle child born in the middle of Generation X. While "Minnesota Nice" is a genuine characteristic trait, it's also a misnomer at times. Minnesotans are nice, but that's often because we are *really good* at keeping our strong opinions to ourselves (especially in a group of transplants). A Minnesotan "Yah, you betcha" can cover a lot of strong opinions underneath.

Being a transplant to the East Coast in the early '90s helped shape how I take in news and current events. When I landed at Boston University in 1994 to embark on a graduate degree in communications, the internet had just started to take hold in academic settings. My class was the first to have an email address. It was a time of many important, breaking news stories:

- The TWA Flight 800 explosion and crash near East Moriches, New York
- Michael Kennedy's affair with his family's sixteen-year-old babysitter and his tragic death in a skiing accident a few months later
- The Waco tragedy from the siege of David Koresh's Branch Davidians
- The Oklahoma City bombing

After graduating from the COM program with a Master of Science degree in communications, a military marriage brought me to Washington,

DC, where I eventually started work as the head of communications for a cruise line. The job provided me with up close experience, navigating the issues impacting the cruise industry from a lobbying perspective. From foreign flagging to fire on cruise ships, the job was perfect for someone who likes to watch events unfold and impact an industry.

Like 9/11.

I could see the Pentagon burn from my office window while I got to work on a crisis plan for the association's cruise line members.

Or like a major, devastating hurricane.

In the Hurricane Katrina fallout, I was working for the Federal Emergency Management Agency (FEMA), in the office of external affairs, working with a team handling post-disaster media efforts.

All these stories and experiences shaped my work in public relations and crisis response.

For decades—centuries, even—the press and media were primarily an analog news service. Network and cable television still captured a lot of eyeballs in the early 2000s; major newspapers still had a lot of readers. But those eyeballs and readers were starting to do something that would turn the traditional media relations model sideways.

With the arrival of the internet—and later, social media—people started commenting on the stories they witnessed play out on television and the newspapers on social media. As Facebook and Twitter went mainstream, so did the idea of adding people's voices to the mix of news stories. Social commentary became a part of the news.

Soon, readers' comments popped up underneath online news stories. The "man on the street" interview morphed into a "man on social media" opinion that found its way into news stories. Reporters would embed live tweets or comments from Facebook to get the public opinion view of a story.

I had always been interested in the public's reaction to news stories, but it was at this moment that my interest in the public's power in shaping news and reputation took hold. I found my hook: tracking how the public shapes news through commentary and then figuring out how to respond to it.

Public opinion is powerful. When a negative groundswell starts online, it is extremely difficult to stop it. One person's opinion begets another. Word of mouth spreads quickly, but it also influences and provokes a public into action. Public opinion can enhance and increase someone's popularity, but it can still knock them down—all within 280 characters or less.

How can businesses and leaders respond the correct way? Is there a way to read the tea leaves and know how an audience is going to respond to an event that spills out online? There's no magic answer, but I've found some tactics to follow a trajectory of a story and predict how it will be received by the public.

I'm no soothsayer, but I do rely on my middle-of-the-road midwestern upbringing, and I have a keen eye for the reaction. After years of watching the reputations of businesses and their leaders, politicians, and formerly unknown people thrust into the spotlight (looking at you, Dr. Palmer), I can read the tea leaves and predict the reaction. Will it happen the way I think it will?

It usually does. Why?

Because any event, crisis, mistake, misdeed, or once-in-a-lifetime incident that hits a brand, business, or leader follows a familiar trajectory. All these events have an inherent chemistry that formulates into a predictable pattern.

It's this pattern of human behavior that I'm drawn to in my work. I am as intrigued by how viral spinouts derail a reputation as I am drawn to helping people prevent it from happening in the first place.

That's why people hire me. I spot risk on the horizon and tell people how to avoid it. If they call me from the middle of a controversy, I help them get out of it as quickly and cleanly as possible.

I have worked at a federal agency, newsrooms, national associations, and television and radio stations. I started work in the time of the beeping fax and now work in a time of tweets and viral videos. As public relations and crisis management has changed drastically in the past two decades, I've been there to witness it and learn from it.

And I've seen the same mistakes repeated again and again. The businesses, brands, and organizations that find themselves in trouble are usually led by executives who misjudge the power of social media and the motives of the public behind it.

After years of speaking to full hotel ballrooms and hotel conference rooms, I observe those mistakes being made on repeat, many times by the smartest people in the room.

The big mistake I notice with business owners, executives, or leaders (anyone who needs public approval or acceptance of their plan, project, business campaign, or work) is *always* the same.

The most dangerous thing a leader can do the moment they hear of pushback from the public is DISMISSAL.

They dismiss the complaint.

They dismiss the complainer.

They dismiss the power of social media.

I have never, EVER worked on or have been aware of a situation in which such dismissal hasn't hurt a business in the short or long run. Whether the damage is extreme or limited, the impact of a public outcry or social media campaign against a person or a business lingers for a long time.

The impact never goes away—exactly like a post on social media. Arrogance mixed with ignorance is a recipe for dismissal—and that's all it takes to start dismantling whatever it is you are trying to build, whether it's a new building or your reputation or your business.

So why do leaders so often dismiss pushback from the public? The number one reason is FEAR.

Fear of consumers rising up against their leadership.

Fear of social media.

Fear of information taken out of context.

Often the greatest threat to an organization comes when they try to avoid a different one. They walk straight into the problem without even knowing it.

KEN FISHER AND THE CLOSED-DOOR MEETING

Billionaire Ken Fisher is a wildly successful money manager. The investment guru has a reputation for being an absolute shark when it comes to making money. He's also got a reputation for being crass and crude and for repeatedly uttering insensitive comments behind closed doors. One particular comment, which compared winning clients to the sexual conquest of women, cost him dearly. That's because one of those business executives he was meeting with, Alex Chalekian, found his behavior abhorrent. In a Twitter rant voicing his displeasure, Chalekian, then forty-three, condemned Fisher's behavior, saying that it left him "truly disgusted."[1]

The result? The video went viral—and the backlash against Fisher was massive. His holding company, Fisher Investments, saw losses in the billions as investors voted with their dollars and pulled their holdings from his company. This was a new territory for Fisher, in his late sixties at the time, who claimed to be surprised his words were considered so offensive, since he'd always talked like that in the past—demonstrating both the type of clueless behavior that tripped him up in the first place and one of the biggest and most prevalent problems in the corporate sector: rampant, institutionalized sexism.

Ken Fisher was not the first executive whose behavior was sorely out of step and who suffered the consequences in the age of #MeToo, and he won't be the last. Fisher's inappropriate remarks behind closed doors represent the initial mistake, but they were compounded when he attempted to skirt the impact of the remarks and offered a rebuke to the backlash. Fisher's response was more or less: "Meh, what's the big deal?" Fisher used a diminishing tactic in the face of the rebuke by trying the excuse that he's been talking that way for years.

Such hubris and naïveté are the key character flaws of a self-destructive leader.

It doesn't matter if you are a leader of a company, organization, or brand. Whether you're a politician, a person in a spotlight, or a relatively unknown leader at a small company, your reputation is your currency. Whether your reach is national or confined to a small town, your reputation is as valuable as it is scarce—you only have one. Managing damage to your reputation is crucial to your long-term viability in your role and in your reputation.

---

1. Darmiento, Laurence. "Ken Fisher Said Money Managers View Winning Clients Like Winning Girls. It Cost Him Big." *Los Angeles Times*, November 7, 2019.

YOUR OWN WORST ENEMY

Unfortunately, managing your reputation online is far more difficult than doing so in person. The people we can see and touch with a handshake or visual explanation can be persuaded or convinced of your remorse if you've been called out for a reputation-damaging incident. Damage control online, however, is an entirely different game. The only tools you have are your words and your social media acumen. If you personally don't have the right skill set, then you must ensure your staff does.

In today's digital age of fast-moving technology and social media, it's challenging for anyone—at any age—to adapt to the rules and protocols of every new social platform. Except for the techies who work deep in the trenches of online technology, the rest of us are left to learn and manage on our own. If you don't have your finger on the pulse of the Byzantine nature of modern technological developments, the questions come fast and hard:

- What type of computer should I be using?
- What is the difference between Android and iOS?
- Will people make fun of me if I still use a flip phone?
- Do I need to be on social media? Can I get by without it and just hire someone to manage it?
- What if someone did say something about me online? Would I know? What would I do if the charges were false?
- Am I the only one who is scared to be in business in the age of social media?

If you can't personally shake the hand of every member of your audience, then this is the book for you. Navigating a social media dustup on your own can be messy. One bad post can ruin your day at best or at worst—ruin your reputation. You need to know the helpful rules to follow, but the good news is that you don't have to be an expert. You do, however, need to be in the proper mindset to learn.

Fighting back against any call-out—regardless of whether it's warranted or not—is like going to war. A key factor in waging any battle is knowing what the enemy knows about you, especially your weaknesses. And if your weakness comes from your values, virtues, or morals, it can create a gap that becomes a major weak point in your defenses, leaving you vulnerable and debilitated. These gaps expose you to your opponent and weaken your position and your ability to fend off reputation-destroying accusations. It's rare for someone who's been through the mud to redeem themselves.

The public and the press usually give a person a second chance. After all, everyone knows the press loves a good second-chance story—reporters love the opportunity to retell all the sordid details of the original incident and then present a new story of redemption, tied up nicely with a bow. Virtues, values, and morals are critical in managing your reputation and becoming an indestructible leader. There are many news stories about people who have found their way online about people falling into reputational death spirals from one wrong decision to use as a cautionary tale. You can follow my playbook to create your indestructible persona, but remember they're only suggestions. Your choices and values are your own. If the choices you make or the public stands you feel you must take don't align with your customers or the public, you may self-destruct.

This playbook isn't going to help anyone who has a moral and ethical compass grossly out of order. However, in today's ever-changing digital environment, there are plenty of skills that any leader can use to become indestructible. If you worry about keeping up with the unpredictability of managing your reputation online (in the good times and the bad), then this is your playbook.

"Being ignorant is not so much a shame, as being unwilling to learn."

—Benjamin Franklin
Poor Richard's Almanac, 1758

CHAPTER 1

YOUR TRUSTED GUIDE

Working as a consultant, workshop facilitator, public speaker, and podcaster, I get to speak with people who span all generations: college students, Baby Boomers, Millennials, and even some seventy-four-year-old directors serving on their organization's board. I work with senior leaders in the C-suite as well as directors in the boardroom. In these face-to-face interactions and in my talks and workshops about public relations, media training, communications, and crisis communications, the conversations eventually turn to technology, social media, and online reputations.

Through my years of work, I have observed more and more people jump into the digital and social game. Five years ago, when I would stand in front of a room of Baby Boomers and ask how many were on Facebook, only one quarter of the room would admit to using the social platform. The remainder would tell me how silly it was to waste time on social media. These same people were proud to whip out their flip phone from their back pocket and tell me that "this thing" was all they needed. (These were always men, by the way. My theory is because women are typically responsible for more schedules, they were quicker to embrace smartphones.)

I notice these disparate opinions every time I stand in a hotel conference room and discuss the impact of social media on a business or organization. I can smell the fear of the older generations as soon as they tell me their excuses for why they would never waste their time on social media.

The Gen Xers and the Millennials? Well, they just sit back and shake their heads. They know better.

There is an absolute line of demarcation between the people who get the need and benefits of social media and those who do not, and never will. You either know how to use the medium in many of its forms to make your life easier and a little more entertaining, or you don't. The people who do know usually understand the problems as well. Social media is an imperfect medium.

For the people who fully embrace the technology, chances are they are what we call Digital Natives. Many of these people grew up with an iPad in their hands at school or at least had access to a computer in their house. Their young minds were wired to grasp the concept of handheld or desktop technology and quickly learned to navigate the features.

What this group doesn't understand, however, is how the older generations feel about using the technology. Although someone in the Baby Boomer or Silent Generation may need a few additional beats to get up-and-running on an iPhone or Dell desktop computer, this group has the ability to master technology the same way as their younger counterparts, perhaps only at a different speed.

It's not how they use technology, necessarily; it's how they feel about it. There is a hesitation due to the unknown of an iPhone's power. It's fear, plain and simple. It's knowing there is a distinct possibility that a person can quickly embarrass themselves online from not understanding the exact protocol of using social media or not knowing where to locate the "kill switch" if the wrong words are used online.

Growing up, this group likely learned from a teacher standing at the front of a room with chalk and a black chalkboard. Assignments were completed on paper using a pencil. Erasing a mistake was as simple as turning the pencil around—the mistake never to be seen again. But there isn't an eraser powerful enough to remove the wrong statement indelibly posted to Twitter by a retweet.

On the one hand, going viral is aspirational for people who seek to build authority online. The publicity! The retweets! Alternatively, viral fame can cost a person dearly if it is damaging to their reputation.

I understand this fear. The internet has opened up wide vistas of possibilities for people and the brands they promote, but navigating this new world can be intimidating. Personally, I distinctly remember the transition from paper to digital. I was at the perfect age (early twenties), in the perfect place (graduate school in Boston), living in the perfect apartment (just behind Fenway Park—Go Red Sox!) and studying for the perfect degree (mass communications with an emphasis on internet studies and news). As a graduate student at Boston University's storied communication school ("COM"), I arrived on campus just as the internet was appearing on the scene. As mentioned earlier, my incoming class in 1993 was the first to have school email addresses. (Mine was "mollybak@bu.ed." This was before email etiquette predicated the first initial, last name combo. Like many others, my first lesson in digital technology was the idea that you just start and learn from there.)

My goal at that time was to find the perfect job that merged news, sales, and the internet. I set my sights on working at a local or national television station. Cable news was just starting to take shape, but at the time, network television had all the juice. My love for news was mixed with the exciting unknown of the internet. But what exhilarated me was knowing that I was onto something—I knew there was potential power for brands and businesses on the internet. Introducing sales was the pragmatic side of me. You needed funds to get this idea off the ground, and advertising sales made perfect sense for introducing news to the internet.

After graduation, I was offered broadcast jobs in newsrooms and sales departments. The former department at the television station wanted me to help put the news online while the latter wanted me to find a way to make money from it.

I tried both, but insufficient knowledge about the online medium and the available budget to support the new venture in the mid-1990s made the job too difficult. Simply put—I was ahead of my time. The want was there to have someone help bring news and ad revenue to the television station's website, but the systems were not. Every station wanted me to work in the sales department. With graduate school loans to pay, I knew the income potential would ease the pain of my upcoming school payments, but my heart wasn't in it. I wanted to work in news and content in this new medium, but the job I was suited for didn't exist yet.

It was about this time I made my second misstep with my career. The head of sales for DoubleClick (an online advertising sales company—I get sick to my stomach just writing this memory) asked me to breakfast in the North End of Boston. I don't remember the restaurant where we ate, but I do remember his pitch for having me work at the startup company that developed and provided ad services for the internet.

I remember wrestling with the decision to abandon my dream of working in broadcast with a job in sales, and in internet sales no less. Where was the excitement? It seemed all so tedious selling ad space on a webpage.

I turned down the job.

Google acquired DoubleClick in 2007.

I try not to think about the alternate Molly who decided to work for DoubleClick. But when I do, I imagine her children's college tuitions are paid for out-of-pocket, she has season tickets down the third-base line at Fenway Park, and is twenty pounds lighter.

Fast-forward to 2007, I (the real me) was working in one of the most traditional environments in the country: the federal government. Um, not exactly DoubleClick acquired by Google.

I was a public affairs specialist—a public relations job for the public sector—working with the Federal Emergency Management Agency. Now this position may not have paid top dollar, but it did give me an amazing opportunity to be the right person at the right disaster, and the person who was just itching to make an impact in a job using social media. But before I could use social media to help save the reputation of the Federal Emergency Management Agency, I accidentally found myself in a position to damage it immensely.

In my first week on the job at FEMA Headquarters, I was summoned to attend a press conference in the agency's main press briefing room where Vice Admiral Harvey E. Johnson Jr., FEMA's deputy administrator, was giving a briefing on the California wildfires. I wasn't told what to do other than to attend and sit in the room. Essentially, a seat filler.

At first, I thought I was in the press room to watch a live press conference as part of my new employee training. When I arrived in the press room, it was me along with a handful of employees working external affairs. I guessed the reporters would arrive later. When Johnson started the press conference, I was confused. Here, the head of the national agency was briefing reporters, but none of the reporters were in the room.

When I asked a colleague where the press was located, they told me they were on the phone. They had to listen to the press briefing on a one-way phone call. No questions were allowed. The briefing was one-way only.

Now, I was really confused.

I'm ashamed to think about it now, but at the time, I do remember feeling like I was the only person in the room who was having trouble digesting the events playing out in front of me in that briefing room. Admiral Johnson kept speaking to reporters from the podium embla-zoned with the FEMA shield, but there were NO REPORTERS IN THE ROOM. Then, he started to take questions from reporters. Er, I mean the FEMA employees. My colleagues were lobbing the questions at Johnson posing as reporters.

Now I knew, without a doubt, the fix I was in. I was witnessing a sham of a press conference, and regrettably, I wasn't doing a thing about it. I did ask one colleague sitting behind me (who I had become friendly with in my first few weeks of work) about the proceedings, but she was more transfixed managing emails in her BlackBerry than participating in the briefing or answering why it was happening in the first place. Like me, she was a seat filler. At one point, I finally found my courage to stand up and yell with my fist in the air, "This press conference is a FARCE!" However, I found the courage stayed in my head. All I could manage was to slightly turn from my seat and move my way to the front, darkened corner of the room to sneak out.

Then, just like that, the briefing was over. I never even stood up. Neither physically nor ethically.

However, what transpired in that briefing room bothered me to the core—and it still does to this day. By the time I got back to my desk on the seventh floor, I was disappointed in myself for not saying anything.

After chewing on it at my desk for a bit, I eventually headed down the hallway to the office of the political appointee in charge of public affairs to discuss what had happened in the briefing room. Before I expressed my concern to him, I asked if what I witnessed was standard operating procedure for a press briefing at FEMA. (I knew it wasn't, but I needed a soft entrance as the new employee). He said, "Oh, yeah—it happens." I only managed to get in a few measly comments why the interactions didn't seem right, and what would happen if a reporter eventually figured out the press conference was fake. I could sense he did not want to talk about the subject any further. As he pooh-poohed my concerns, I took my cue and left his office.

It wasn't long before someone did notice that a certain official press conference was not as official as it appeared.

Al Kamen—a now-retired *Washington Post* reporter who, frankly many felt, had it in for FEMA—published the story of the fake press conference. The headline, a nod to the late Tim Russert's Sunday morning program, was "FEMA Meets the Press, Which Happens to be FEMA." The article included all the gritty details from the briefing and was accompanied by a photograph with the names of all the FEMA employees seated in the briefing room, save one: me. I was listed as "an unidentified employee." That was a clue as to the identity of the mole employed at FEMA who leaked the photo to *The Washington Post*. Everyone working in external affairs knew who I was by name, but apparently not everyone at FEMA, or at least not the mole.

The fact that I had dodged a reputational bullet made the whole ordeal a little more tolerable, but the whole sordid affair still gnawed at me. The fake briefing was wrong, and I knew it was wrong, but I didn't say anything. The situation did not go away with one story in *The Washington Post* about a fake press briefing. When the story broke nationally a few days later, it went viral before "going viral" was even a thing. When your first weeks on the job are portrayed in a cold open on *Saturday Night Live,* you know it can only go uphill from there.

Yes, FEMA had a few bungled PR moments, but they sadly distracted from the admirable work from well-meaning and respected employees at the agency. I never regretted working there a single day—okay, twenty minutes of a press briefing, sure—and I loved the work and the colleagues with whom I still communicate to this day. Like many government agencies, FEMA had its fair share of political dead weight appointees, but most of my colleagues at the agency sought to find ways to help victims of natural disasters recover as quickly as humanly possible. Unlike many agencies in Washington, DC, we saw that the work we were doing paid off every time someone received aid to help them back on their feet. It was rewarding work, and I never tired of doing it, even when it was challenging and exhausting—such as when I was tasked with handling the infamous "FEMA formaldehyde trailers" issue in January 2007, shortly after Hurricane Katrina.

FEMA had provided temporary trailers for many of the people displaced by the storm to live in. For a region decimated by the hurricane, these trailers were a relief to the thousands of people who were flooded out of homes or whose towns were completely destroyed. These FEMA trailers were a lifesaver until they weren't—and FEMA had another crisis waiting.

It was found the trailers had increased levels of formaldehyde—the chemical you find in nail polish remover and embalming fluid. *That* was certainly picked up on when the press reported the story. From a public affairs perspective, it was a difficult story to message because it was true; the trailers did have formaldehyde, but that was true of most recreational vehicles and trailers. What made this issue problematic was that people were staying in the trailers for an extended period of time, much longer than they were designed for. These temporary trailers were deemed temporary residences, but the occupants were starting to get sick. FEMA once again was put in a problematic situation and was on the wrong side of the story. My job was getting more challenging by the day.

Katrina had left New Orleans underwater and destroyed a considerable area along the Gulf Coast. The hurricane caused significant damage to the agency as well. The press and other figureheads were relentless in their attacks against FEMA for botching the response efforts. When thousands were left stranded in the Superdome (now known as the Mercedes-Benz Superdome), FEMA took the hit. The blame was not misplaced; FEMA did indeed botch much of the response efforts. But let's just say there was plenty of blame to go around. Hurricane Katrina was one of those "Black Swan" or unknown or unpredictable events that no one saw coming. All the agencies—federal, state, and local—were caught off guard when the storm made landfall in September 2006.

All it took was the turn of one phrase, uttered by President George Bush about FEMA Administrator Michael Brown, to send the agency into a tailspin. "Heck of a job, Brownie," became synonymous with massive bureaucratic failures.

My job at the agency almost a year later was to try to undo that image, to project the agency in a favorable light and try to garner as much positive press as I could from my role, first as a public affairs specialist and then as the news manager working in external affairs. The job wasn't easy because we were the laughingstock of Washington. No one in the press would take my calls, yet story after story maligned the agency. The DC press corps and seemingly everyone else was out to get us.

On the one hand, the work was rewarding. From my position at FEMA headquarters, I could see firsthand all the important work the agency was doing to help people suffering through a natural disaster. During my time with FEMA, I worked on wildfires, tornadoes, hurricanes, tropical storms, and flooding. You don't realize how many disasters truly impact Americans until you have to respond to the disaster in the day-to-day of your job. FEMA resources were triggered as soon as the president of the United States declared it a federal disaster. Once the disaster was declared, then each agency was put to work to help the victims recover.

Yet in February 2008, I had about had it with the collective bashing from the press. I couldn't get a reporter to take a positive story from FEMA if my life depended on it. I knew there was a better way to tell the positive work FEMA was doing. In my role working with individual assistance, I was hearing firsthand from the people we were helping. Daily I would speak to someone new who would thank me profusely for getting them the funds to get back on their feet, for finding a hotel for them to stay in while their town was flooded—you name it. This was a frustrating dichotomy that happened constantly. I knew there must be a way around the scorn of the press. All it took was to go back to my graduate school days at COM to find the answer. If the press didn't want to report on our side of the story, well then—who says we couldn't tell it ourselves?

This is where my age, my background, and developing technology aligned beautifully. In 2007, the internet (still "the Internet" with a capital *I* at that point) was an important communication channel, but the flow of information was largely unilateral. Organizations put all the information the public wanted to find on a website, halfway between a news outlet and the Yellow Pages. There were chat rooms and email, but social media was still relatively novel in Washington, DC. Facebook was a channel for college campuses, not for the public, and especially not for people in the Beltway.

I proposed to deploy myself to the next federally declared disaster as a backpack journalist. Armed with a camera and a mic, I could interview the types of people I usually encountered over the phone when they needed individual assistance. I immediately got the OK from my open-minded FEMA supervisor Marty Bahamonde and I patiently waited for the next disaster. When reports were indicating straight-line winds and tornadoes were headed toward Tennessee and Arkansas, so was I. I grabbed my go-to media bag and was off. (Not before I had to prep and organize for four kids to be at home—all under the age of six—with Dad for a spell. With one parent working at FEMA and the other heading media relations at US Coast Guard headquarters, we knew the art of a juggle.)

After I landed at Memphis International Airport and rented a car, I set out with only one task on my to-do list: Find victims from the storm who need help from FEMA.

The tornadoes were dubbed the 2008 Super Tuesday tornado outbreak because it began on Super Tuesday when twenty-four states were holding primary elections for the upcoming presidential election. Over two days, eighty-seven tornadoes caused massive destruction and killed a total of fifty-seven people across four states.

At the time of these storms in 2008, mobile communications came from a BlackBerry. The only means to find the destruction from the tornadoes was to ask people who survived them. I knew which counties took the brunt of the storms, but it was up to me to find the people affected by them.

I chose to head into the direction of Jackson, Tennessee, where a violent EF4 tornado touched down and destroyed parts of town, including damaging buildings located on the Union University campus.

I drove to the first mobile FEMA station I could find and introduced myself to the disaster assistance employees (DAEs) assigned to the recovery effort. They were eager to help me with my interviews as much as they were to help the people of Jackson. DAEs were temporary employees who traveled to federally declared disasters—sometimes back-to-back—to help disaster victims. These employees are a valuable resource to the agency.

I interviewed countless people my first day at the disaster, both FEMA employees and displaced people in Jackson. However, no one was completely comfortable opening up to me on camera. I wasn't surprised.

Abrupt displacement from a severe storm would leave anyone vulnerable. This wasn't an ideal time to get people to open up to me; I felt no different from a television reporter in search of the "if it leads, it bleeds" soundbite.

After my first day on the ground, I accumulated hours of interviews but was still in search of the right person to talk to on camera. I wasn't sure what exactly I was looking for, but I knew it had something to do with authenticity.

The next morning, she appeared. A young mother who looked to be in her mid-twenties looking exhausted and a little lost. I approached her. First, I asked how she was coping and what help she needed. She told me her home received significant damage from the storm, and she wasn't sure how to get through the FEMA process. She told me after the storm died down, she had stepped onto her dark street to look for help. Her neighbors told her to find FEMA.

That's what brought her to this line talking to me.

My concern was to make sure she and her two young children were safe and had a place to sleep. She told me everyone was safe, including her mother who lived with the family. My heart was tugging in the right place just as my mind was adjusting to the opportunity in front of me. This displaced mother who aspired to be a nurse was calm, articulate, and unashamed of asking for help when she needed it. She was the perfect subject for my video.

I accompanied her as she filled out her FEMA assistance forms and then I followed her home in my car. When I arrived, the scene was heartbreaking. The modest home was halved by an enormous tree right down the middle—their belongings scattered everywhere in the yard.

She was so gracious to share her experience with FEMA to me on video. The best person to interview for any piece of communications collateral is someone with authenticity. The more genuine and the more honest a person can be on video, the more valuable the video becomes.

I interviewed numerous people in Tennessee over the course of those days, but my young mother was by far the best. Her youth meant a familiarity with technology and video that allowed me to capture an authentic experience with FEMA.

After a few days on the ground, I flew back to Washington, DC, and got straight to editing the hours of interviews with two colleagues who were the AV wizards of FEMA. Aaron Skolnik and Paul Luke sat with me for a few days while we compiled and edited the video to create a presentation that would set the direction of my career for over the next decade.

As I sat down with them to edit the video, I did not know exactly what the end product was going to look like. The only direction I could give them was that I did not want a documentary. What I wanted was a series of clips we could post to the FEMA website that told one story, but in several, consecutive clips. I didn't realize it at the time, but I was on my way to creating FEMA's first social media narrative.

Once the mini-films of my young mother were finished, I presented a plan for a reputational rehabilitation for the agency to all the heads of external affairs (as well as the heads of the ten regional offices around the country) by pitching an internal communication plan for changing the public opinion of FEMA's external audiences. My colleague in external affairs, John Shea, joined me as we presented a new direction for how the agency could manage the press, by distributing our news ourselves. By filming and producing our content, in essence, we could bypass the negative press with reporters who appeared to have a bias against the agency for overlooking the admirable work of the agency and only focusing on the bad. This online concept was not a propaganda project, but a way to use a powerful emerging medium to promote the good work being overlooked.

The videos changed public affairs for FEMA. The videos also changed my fortunes because the person who greenlit the trip for me had another offer up his sleeve. This time, Marty Bahamonde asked me to head up social media for FEMA.

I was thrilled to be at the forefront of a new channel for communications—social media. The possibility of heading the online efforts at FEMA was a job designed for no one but ME! It was going to be the perfect job to become a thought leader in the area of social and emergency management. That is, until it wasn't. Duty called—again. A military transfer upended our family—we were sent off to Portland, Maine. I had to move away from yet another job I loved.

Over the next few months, my sad task was to ramp up the person following me in the social media job, but thankfully FEMA took care of me by giving me a Disaster Workforce Division (DAE) position. Even better, I could begin my deployment remotely online, monitoring disasters online from home. The position would have been perfect but for one minor aspect—I had to monitor and then compile press reports for distribution at the morning external affairs briefing. One notable disaster at that time was DR-1791, which stands for the disaster declaration and recovery number for Hurricane Ike.

These "hot sheets" had to be finished by the start of the 8 a.m. meeting, which meant I was working paperboy hours to deliver the news. And then there was that slight juggle of getting four kids under the age of eight to two separate schools in two towns that were in opposite directions from one another!

I was grateful for the work, but I missed my old position terribly. FEMA fortune came knocking a few months later. A "broadcast task force" of sorts was being assembled to film FEMA's preparedness efforts before storms caused any damage. It was a proactive communications strategy to show the agency's transparency after the Hurricane Katrina fallout as well as the extreme efforts FEMA was taking to prevent another one. The team was assembled just as a storm brewing off the mid-Atlantic coast.

The team was tasked with documenting the efforts in the joint information centers—where all the federal, state, and local public affairs officers worked before and after the storm.

Even better, I would be working with two colleagues from headquarters—public affairs coworker John Shea would serve as an executive producer of sorts and the formidable photographer Jocelyn Augustino would take photos. Another DAE from Florida, Michael Moore, would serve as a videographer, and I would work as a producer/reporter. Our job was to cover the approaching storm, soon to be named Tropical Storm Hannah, as it worked its way toward North Carolina.

I kissed my kids goodbye and told them I would be back much sooner than a typical US Coast Guard deployment. They knew the drill, which made the trip easier to make, but I would definitely miss my family. This was the longest I was ever going to be away from the kids.

The trip started out smoothly. We all met in Washington, DC, and headed south to track the storm. We had excellent weather reports, so we knew exactly how far ahead we needed to travel to film the preparation efforts before the storm (which is also the coolest time to watch a storm—the job was getting better and better).

We landed in North Carolina, headed in our two cars to Elizabeth City first, then all four of us made our way to Station Wilmington Beach, where the US Coast Guard station was making preparations for Tropical Storm Hannah.

Not surprisingly, no one was on high alert just yet. After all, the weather still felt like a summer beach day, even though we were a week into September. Despite the placid weather, we had to start filming our tropical storm footage of the FEMA efforts. After speaking with the team back at headquarters, John set up our trips and planned what we needed to film. We were making our way through South Carolina on our way to Georgia when the tropical storm hit the Southeast coast and the Gulf of Mexico. We filmed some at the Joint Information Center (JIC) in Georgia; I especially remember filming semitrucks filled with water and other provisions that were provided by Walmart in the new private sector partnership started at the agency.

As the film crew responsible for filming the preparation efforts of the storm, it was important that my team of four kept ahead of it. This time-table prevented us from feeling the full effect of Hannah, but we had a bigger storm to deal with in Tropical Storm Ike, which was closing in on the Gulf states. At the time, the storm was tracking similarly to Hurricane Katrina, and our handlers told us that documenting the preparation and restoration efforts would be the focal task of the trip.

We drove most of the night to get to Texas in time. Our first official stop in Texas was in San Antonio to meet with the Federal Coordinating Officers and the Urban Task Force guys (they were all guys back then). These are firefighters and other emergency rescue personnel who are specially trained in emergency rescue during natural disasters. I was tasked with giving these FEMA employees some media training in preparation for the television, radio, and print interviews. Pre- and post-storm were the golden hours for getting good press at FEMA.

With the storm heading quickly toward the eastern coast of Texas, we needed to head back to Houston and get situated in our hotel before Ike, now a hurricane, hit. We checked into the hotel and headed up to bed to wait for Ike to hit Houston. I fell asleep in bed and woke up a few hours later with Category 3 winds lashing at the windows to my room on the eighteenth floor.

In the hours after Hurricane Ike made landfall, we made our way to the areas hardest hit by the storm. Mike and I partnered up and drove toward Corpus Christie. We were one of the few cars on the road; it was a little nerve-wracking because most of the gas stations were empty, and our car would soon be as well if we didn't find a station that had gas available.

This was a time before GPS-enabled smartphones—*I barely remember such a time*—but we had to chart our trip with a map, cell phones, and a lot of luck. Our first stop to set up shop to begin filming response efforts was in Orange, Texas. The shelter for emergency personnel was a middle school gymnasium. Hundreds of emergency management personnel jammed into a space with no power, no showers, no air conditioning—and it was as awful as it sounds. Mike and I filmed and reported all day in the hot and muggy swamp areas around Orange and came back to the sweltering shelter. The conditions were awful, and we were exhausted, but the work itself was rewarding.

Mike filmed the Urban Rescue Guys while I interviewed them. Wherever FEMA told us to go and film, we went. When they weren't telling us where to go, we would find our own place to film. There was plenty of destruction to witness. I came to regret not wearing my boots before I got stuck in swampy land on our last day in Orange, Texas. My hiking shoes were soaked and caked with mud. Thankfully, we were headed back to Houston again—back to electricity and hot showers—but those muddy shoes would come back to haunt me.

The next day in Houston we met up with Jocelyn and John and started filming the FEMA efforts in Houston. Around noon, we met a FEMA satellite truck in the parking lot of a nearby Baptist church. Mike and I were tasked with filming and interviewing people waiting in line in their vehicles. No foot traffic was allowed because FEMA was giving out pallets of water and ice, making it too difficult for people to walk home carrying them. There were police on hand to handle the traffic. As the people of Houston vied for supplies, tempers began to flare. Having spent a few days in a sweaty gymnasium with no electricity, I had a lot of empathy for these residents. Working on the hot asphalt was painful and exhausting. Mike was lugging the video camera—and it was the size of a television news camera, mounted on the shoulder, not easy to bear for an extended period of time. I offered to film for him while he cooled off in the trailer. Plus, I wanted to get behind the camera to take a break from talking to the impatient people waiting in line. It wasn't a particularly fun story to report. There weren't any soundbites to be had. These people were hot, tired, and in need of water.

As I was filming, the footage was streamed from the satellite truck live and watched by my colleagues in the van, as well as by Aaron and Paul working in the studio at FEMA headquarters in Washington, DC.

With the camera on my shoulder, I remember feeling a jolt of sympathy for Mike having to lug this camera around the entire trip. It was heavy. Since we were moving around so much, it was impractical to haul around a tripod, so we steadied ourselves filming by spreading our legs out wide for balance. This balance maneuver required stable shoes. However, since my hiking shoes were caked with (now-dry) mud and the weather was sweltering (which had ruled out my wading boots), I had to wear my one remaining pair of shoes—sandals.

As I stood on the pavement filming in my sandals, I heard yelling behind me. I could hear a conversation between a police officer standing off to the side of me with a man in his vehicle. The conversation was getting testy enough that I could tell it was escalating between the two men, but not enough to stop me from my filming.

As I filmed, I heard more yelling and then the ominous sound of screeching tires.

Ominous, because I knew the sound was behind me and also coming at me. The next thing I knew, I felt a terrible jolt. Heard a thud—the camera—and then silence. That deadly frightful silence when no one wants to acknowledge what happened because no one is entirely sure what did happen.

I was now on the ground; the wind was knocked out of my lungs. The camera was a few feet from my reach, still filming and streaming live, and pointed at me. The video was capturing me on the ground with my leg wedged under the front tire of a large van.

This was one of those out-of-body experiences you hear about when people recall almost-deadly events that happen to them.

Recalling now from firsthand experience, it's as if the body is slowing down for your brain to catch up to what has happened to you. On the one hand, I knew the van that stopped on my leg left me temporarily immobile. I also knew if I tried to jiggle my leg free, it would likely cause a lot more damage. Damage I could not pinpoint at that moment due to shock. I was calm, but I knew that feeling would soon change as my body started to register the pain. The police officer immediately came to my aid, but there was nothing he could do since I was lodged underneath the van.

When I couldn't extricate myself, panic slowly started to creep in. At first, I noticed the new hole in my work khakis and wondered if they were still usable when I reported back to work later in the day. How many days would this accident set me back for my marathon training? Would I even be able to run a marathon?

As the minutes crept by slowly with no plan to move the van off my leg, the fear quickly escalated from my marathon training to the possibility of severely damaging, perhaps losing, my leg.

Like many PR crises, no one had a plan at the onset of my crisis. How do you extricate a person lodged under a van? Do you drive it off a person or gather a group of strong people to lift it? One objective the police officer recognized needed to happen was to get the eight people sitting in the van out of it without me noticing.

There were eight people in that van. I knew that number because I felt every jostle and jump out the door each time an occupant left the vehicle. With every jump, the leather from the strap dug deeper into the skin between my big toe and the next one.

Even after the driver jumped out of the front seat, his vehicle was still on my leg. No one was doing anything to remove it. They tried to lift the vehicle off my leg, but to no avail. I knew the only option left was going to be a painful one. The officer told the driver to jump back in the van and move it off my leg. Now I was in a full panic.

Meanwhile, less than twenty yards away in the FEMA satellite truck, my colleagues weren't even aware of the situation. It took Aaron and Paul in DC to tell them a van hit me. Aaron and Paul raised the alarm bell so quickly and so effectively that my FEMA coworker and good friend Debbie Wing was calling me on my BlackBerry while the van was still on top of me. She told me later that people at headquarters heard I was intentionally run over by a driver who hated FEMA and wanted to take out one of its workers. Gulp.

Needless to say, I let the call from Debbie go to voicemail.

At this point, I remember a number of other FEMA employees and colleagues making their way to me. Mike, distressed and confused, grabbed the camera from the ground. I recall him saying to me, "I just left you like ten minutes ago. What happened?!"

The van happened.

I can still feel the weight of the driver's body as he got back into the van. It sank down even deeper on me. The pain had become unbearable at this point—the thought of him peeling out on my leg terrified me.

The drive off the leg felt a lot worse than the drive on. I expected to see a crushed bloody leg underneath. But it actually turned out to be fine. The doctor told me all that marathon training I had been doing paid off. My foot, however, had seen better days. It was intact, but multiple bones were crushed and shattered. As they loaded me into the ambulance, I knew my job was finished, over. My spirit was as crushed as my foot. I knew I would never have a job like that again.

At the hospital, I received X-rays, stitches, and a temporary cast and crutches. After that, it was a complete blur. I remember every stop on the trip to Houston, but I have no memory whatsoever of the way home. I know I flew home, and that's about it—now I was without a job, and I was living in Portland, Maine. I knew the road was going to be a rough one. I never did make it to that marathon. My running days were over. So was the broadcast strike team concept.

It was determined the accident was not intentional by the driver, but the result was that FEMA headquarters, I'm told, thought the concept was too risky for employees. My broadcasting days were over, but there was a new medium waiting for me to tackle just around the corner.

My time at FEMA had given me a new vision. I was no longer going to help people shape their reputations from a media-relations perspective; I was on my way to help leaders and their organizations learn how to shape reputations from a public perspective.

Without a doubt, I was at the wrong place and at the wrong time when I was standing in the parking lot broadcasting for FEMA, but it was at the right time to start formulating a plan for organizations and its leaders to learn how to navigate messaging in an online environment. How not to overreact when people react to your business online. How to respond when a controversy you are tied up in goes viral. How to approach using online messaging and social media amplification to shape your story while helping the press react favorably to you.

In other words, how not to get run over.

CHAPTER 2

HOW WE GOT HERE

The Historical and Technical Changes that Rewrote the Rules for CEOs

It wasn't supposed to be like this for a CEO.

Flashback to a captain of industry in the mid-twentieth century, handling a public relations crisis. He (invariably the CEO was male) hid from the public in his mahogany-lined office. His secretary shielded him from unwanted intrusions. His PR man gave reporters a polished press release just in time to meet their deadlines.

What happened? What forces have made that image all but impossible to imagine now?

Here's my highly condensed, slightly opinionated version.

THE UNQUESTIONED CEO

From the dawn of the industrial era, business leaders assumed an almost unquestioned sense of authority. They drove the economic powerhouses that provided jobs, goods, and services. And for the most part, the public ceded their rights to question them, save for the union leaders who battled them for better wages and working conditions. The CEO had little interest in engaging the public personally. Consumer loyalty was to a brand name. The CEO's identity was largely irrelevant. As long as the economy was healthy and the middle class growing more prosperous, there was little incentive to learn about those anonymous men in their mahogany-walled offices.

The public's hunger to learn more about prominent personalities was largely confined to entertainers and, to a lesser extent, politicians. The Hollywood PR machine crafted stories about their stars that portrayed them as wholesome, clean, and upright, no matter the reality. Bad behavior was covered up, and the mainstream press was happy to oblige. A subcategory of tabloids and gossip rags tried to capitalize on the stars' shortcomings, but those publications were held in low esteem by a majority, somewhere in the vicinity of girlie magazines, "true crime" stories, and pulp fiction. *The New York Times*' slogan drew the line: "All the news that's fit to print." And if the press knew that a US president was suffering physical maladies or was unfaithful to his wife, well, that wasn't deemed worth sharing with readers.

But then the '60s happened.

THE DIMINISHMENT OF AUTHORITY FIGURES

The Vietnam War sparked massive resistance and demonstrations by young people who decided this war wasn't a cause worth dying for. The counterculture solidified a generational break from what was labeled "The Establishment" and the roles expected of them. The civil rights and feminist movements gave a voice to large segments of society who had previously been marginalized. Baby Boomers came to doubt the wisdom of their elders and public figures, encapsulated in the dictum, "Question authority." With Watergate and the resignation of President Richard Nixon, the decline of faith in traditional leadership had begun.

The people who led the nascent political movements didn't look like the older leaders; they were women and people of color—not just Martin Luther King, but Malcolm X, Cesar Chavez, Angela Davis, Gloria Steinem, and a host of others. What's more, the new leaders and their followers had proven they could affect social change. With marches, boycotts, and other actions that drew press attention to their causes, they spurred the passage of legislation favorable to their causes and shifted societal norms.

The younger generation's near-universal loss of respect for "The Establishment" extended to an array of institutions too. Law enforcement, the military, political parties, corporations, and religious entities all were subject to criticism and rejection in ways that would have been unfathomable in the conformist era of the 1950s.

THE RISE OF PERSONALITY CULTURE

In the midst of all the negativity about institutions and traditional leaders, the focus shifted to the individual. Author Tom Wolfe dubbed the Boomers the "Me Generation" as a criticism of their narcissism. The fascination with the individual extended to publications. *People* magazine arrived in 1974, limiting its coverage to those in the news rather than the news itself. Similar magazines such as *In Touch* and *Us Weekly* popped up shortly thereafter, beginning a rise of celebrity culture and softening the line between the tabloids and mainstream media.

In the same decade, Lee Iacocca, the CEO of Chrysler who had led its successful bailout in Congress, made himself the star in a long campaign of television commercials. His closing refrain, "If you can find a better car, buy it," restored enough faith in the carmaker for Chrysler to survive. Others successfully tapped into the CEO-as-pitchman ad formula, including Dave Thomas of Wendy's, and Victor Kiam, who said he liked Remington so much that he bought the company. Eventually Steve Jobs would develop a unique and powerful method for promoting Apple, introducing new products in front of live audiences while wearing his daily uniform of a black turtleneck and jeans—not exactly traditional CEO garb.

Unsurprisingly, Iacocca, Thomas, Kiam, and Jobs were all subjects of *People* magazine coverage.

The personality culture spilled over into politics too. Jimmy Carter gained attention not because he was so well-regarded for his accomplishments as a Georgia governor, but because he was a Washington outsider, modestly describing himself as a "peanut farmer." Ronald Reagan was an actor whose fame first helped him win the governorship of California, then the presidency.

The line between what was off the record and what was fair game was further blurred when presidential candidate Gary Hart challenged reporters to prove rumors of his infidelity by spying on his daily activities. They did, found evidence to support the rumors, and ended his candidacy. A decade later, Bill Clinton was on television, denying claims of an affair with an intern: "I did not have sex with that woman." It was a position no president had been put in before, although history suggests many of them held extramarital affairs while in office. The press simply looked the other way and no one else dared raise the issue.

THE ARRIVAL OF GAME-CHANGING TECHNOLOGY

The final piece of the puzzle came during the Clinton era: the World Wide Web. With the internet accessible and understandable to the public, the foundation was laid for a digital revolution and all its far-reaching effects. Primitive at first, the online world began shifting informational power away from its long-established concentration in newspapers, magazines, radio, and television. Desktop publishing had given consumers a glimpse of do-it-yourself communications. With the web, they started creating the digital counterparts. And if they didn't want to invest the time and energy to do so, they could at minimum communicate with others instantly through the new tool called "email."

Progressive new mobile phones amped up the use of email, allowing instant, inexpensive sharing of information. With the arrival of the iPhone and its Android-based equivalents in 2007, the power shifted further. Now millions of ordinary citizens could photograph or videotape events and share them widely. If newsworthy enough, they became the raw material for traditional media outlets.

To cite one example, consider newsmaker Scott Prouty. Doesn't ring a bell? Prouty was a bartender at a function in which presidential candidate Mitt Romney was speaking in 2012. Surreptitiously placing his smartphone in a position to record the speech, Prouty recorded Romney's disparaging remarks about the forty-seven percent of the electorate who would always vote for President Obama because they depended on government entitlement programs. Prouty passed along the recording to a magazine, effectively ending Romney's hopes to unseat the incumbent.

All it took to change the course of history was an iPhone in proximity of a candidate who was none the wiser. This integration between technology and viral media was transforming crisis response. Anyone not paying attention to actions being captured on a smartphone would learn when it came time to release an official response: they were limited to one choice—the truth. Technology doesn't often lie.

THE ECONOMIC WILD CARD

In large measure, CEOs and the corporations they ran weren't questioned in earlier eras because the wealth they created was beneficial to their workers. Henry Ford deliberately paid his factory workers higher wages so they could afford to buy his new Model T. A thriving middle class grew from the post-war economic boom as factories ran at full bore and American goods dominated foreign trade. With globalization, those factory jobs have largely disappeared. Wages have stagnated for a sizable portion of American workers or decreased significantly, especially with the economic downturn due to the Coronavirus pandemic. While the country has continued to grow and unemployment is low, there's no denying that the American dream has faded for millions. Anger and resentment of those earning more, fear of diminishing control over their lives, and loss of employment opportunities in rural communities—it all adds up to a boiling pot, ready to blow its lid in any direction.

And social media is one of the easiest ways to let off steam. In some circumstances, it can cause an explosion that seriously damages a resented institution and its leadership. All these changes in communication now make it easier than ever for one individual to rally hundreds or thousands or even millions to a cause.

The secretary trying to block outsiders from reaching the CEO has been permanently circumvented. Now, anyone and everyone can get to the CEO, even indirectly, by demanding an answer to something they witnessed.

Recall the 2017 episode in which a passenger was dragged off an overbooked United Airlines flight while fellow passengers videotaped the whole thing and shared it on social media. It brought a quick condemnation from politicians, including President Trump. What did United CEO Oscar Munoz do? He issued a statement justifying the forceful removal of the passenger, whom he described as "belligerent." Contradicted by witnesses, Munoz corrected himself two days later in a subsequent release. Munoz had been in line to be designated chairman of United. After the way he handled the removal incident, he was denied that promotion.

The historical forces and technological changes have altered almost everything about life as we know it, and that means CEOs can't hide behind a mahogany desk and a gatekeeper secretary anymore.

Back when I was the director of communications for the cruise association in Arlington, Virginia, one of my primary responsibilities was to draft talking points for each one of the issues affecting the cruise lines industry. In another way of putting it, I instructed anyone speaking for the association how to respond to the raw areas: crime, environment, foreign flagging, cruise line safety, employment, taxes, and safety. I researched the facts, crafted the talking points, and then distributed them to the president and other vice presidents who were often tapped to speak to the press about specific issues. The areas were sticky ones for the industry, so it was best to stay on message. My role back in the early 2000s was no different than anyone else's in the same position. When we spoke to the press, a spokesperson could deliver a quote or statement for direct attribution—from the spokesperson—or indirect attribution by stating it came from someone else (usually the head of the organization). It was an accepted practice that helped reporters get their quotes in enough time to write their stories before the deadline—which, in the time before social media, meant when the printing press started rolling or when the news went on the air.

What this also meant for leaders in a time before social media was an acknowledged and accepted barrier of protection from the time the press asked for a comment or interview. The beneficial protection of time meant leaders could vet statements and have talking points prepared that mitigated the risk of talking themselves into trouble.

That was then.

Social media has upended the media relations cycle. Reporters' deadlines are now rolling. The daily print deadlines are still in the 4:00–5:00 p.m. range, and the national and local news stations need stories produced for and live shots ready for an evening newscast. However, with the twenty-four-hour news cycle, it's no surprise reporters need news stories that are not only accurate and properly sourced but also need to have a viral quality that makes people want to click and open. For the reporter's part—why waste time waiting on a call from an intermediary when you can send a direct message (DM) or tag a person on social media or send an email to the head of an organization? Social media created a direct line of communication expectation. If a reporter asks a question on social media for an organization to respond to and no one from said organization answers, then what?

Silence.

Then that silence is filled with commentary from the public, and then—before you know it—the cancel culture is born.

Leaders who understand that the vacuum needs to be filled with their cooperation with reporters can operate and live in a culture of mutual and beneficial relationships with the press and the public.

Conversely, the leaders who continue to shield themselves from questions that need responding put themselves at risk of being shut down or cancelled.

CHAPTER 3

HEY! YOU'VE BEEN CANCELLED

The call-out culture and cancel culture—they're essentially two descriptions of the same movement—is a movement that's critical to understand in the business of online reputation management.

Call-Out Culture is the concept of a group of people—"the culture"—who feel the need to "call people out" for a misdeed or a failure to acknowledge that misdeed. This new trend in social activism focuses on drawing attention to the perceived negative behavior of major public entities. The people who make up this culture are comfortable giving and receiving feedback. They grew up in a social media generation of likes and dislikes. In other words, they can stand the heat in the kitchen. They have parents who likely chided them for "putting your whole life on social media."

The person who lives in this culture is as comfortable with feedback as they are savvy using social media. Yes, it can be used as a weapon, but it often starts as a query for other like-minded people: "Folks, is there something more to this? What do you think?" When the like-minded start to congregate on a subject, they feel even more confident calling out the perceived offender. This call-out momentum starts the ball rolling into the next phase: cancellation.

Cancel Culture goes beyond baring a target's perceived sins to the world. Most cancel culture campaigns against a public figure also have an activist component, where they urge consumers to cancel their participation with or support for a public figure. As a result of being "cancelled," the public figure often loses not only their reputation but their income as well.

In action, cancel culture is a direct result of the internet and mobile connectivity. Ideas, concepts, images, and videos can all be shared around the globe in a flash, and that allows a campaign to "cancel" a public entity to grow and flourish in no time at all. This speed has given cancel culture its immense clout, as it puts the power in the hands of countless consumers and public citizens across the globe.

Although the trend is fairly recent, the idea of being cancelled is not. Individuals have been shamed and ostracized for violating a social contract throughout human history. The concept is real and timeless. The purpose of the cancel culture today is to position oneself on a particular side of the issue and then find and cultivate an online army of like-minded people. As Adrian Vermeule Tyler, professor of Constitutional Law at Harvard Law School, tweeted:

> "'Cancel culture' just means defining what is unacceptable within the city and, in the limit, who should be expelled from the city. Every culture is a cancel culture. If you don't like progressive cancel culture, what you don't like is just the content of what is cancelled."[1]

EXACTLY HOW DO YOU END UP CANCELLED?

In a world where millennials and Generation Z have watched the decisions of Baby Boomers destroy the environment and the economy with apparently zero repercussions, their anger and resentment has grown strong. It's reasonable to assume that cancel culture stems from the younger generations who respond to older generations with the sarcastic phrase, "OK, Boomer."

---

1. Vermeule, Adrian. Twitter Post. September 19, 2019, 7:27 PM. https://twitter.com/Vermeullarmine/status/1174857529878298624.

Having grown up with mobile technology and social media, Millennials and Gen Z organize and interact over the internet with ease. The internet has given these generations a voice, and it has empowered them to use that voice. However, it's a mistake to assume that only the younger people cause all this turmoil online. The culture has been formed by people of *all* ages who are comfortable speaking out online. It's a mistake to assume the only people speaking out online are Millennials and their younger counterparts.

I hear these complaints about Millennials from leaders from another generation over and over again:

"They are lazy!"

"They're narcissists who only care about themselves!"

"They're not loyal to anyone!"

"Whenever I see a Millennial, they have a phone in their hands!"

When I hear it in person during a talk or workshop I am conducting, the leaders' dismissal of the younger generations' complaints ranges from nonchalance to seething anger.

Assuming these cultures are limited to a certain age group is a fatal mistake for any person in any business to make. It's essential to understand that any culture is formed by a variety of people, united by their shared ideas and shared desire for change. While younger people tend to be more proficient with social media call outs and cancellations, it is the mindset—not the age set—that brings someone or something down.

This idea of empowering cultures striking back at the status quo has resulted in movements like the #MeToo movement,[2] which holds perpetrators of rape, sexual violence, or sexually inappropriate behavior responsible for their actions. The fall of media mogul Harvey Weinstein[3] is perhaps the most notable result of the movement, proving that such tactics can indeed change the world for the better and bring justice to those wronged. All it takes is a single social media post to gain traction by being

---

2. "About." Me Too Movement. Accessed February 14, 2020. https://metoomvmt.org/about.

3. Kantor, Jodi, and Megan Twohey. "Harvey Weinstein Paid Off Sexual Harassment Accusers for Decades." *The New York Times*, October 5, 2017. https://www.nytimes.com/2017/10/05/us/harvey-weinstein-harassment-allegations.html.

shared far and wide and, avalanche-like, a movement gains momentum and barrels down, crushing everything in its wake.

Those who are threatened by this cancel culture tend to grow weary of the mentality and try to dismiss it as a "youthquake" movement of destruction. They cling to the hope this movement's fifteen minutes of fame are soon to be up and the next wave of destruction is waiting to replace it.

If someone created a virtual cancel culture time capsule, it would be labeled 2019, the year the term went mainstream. Many of the people who faced the shame mobs during that year were usually caught flat-footed by the blowback from the shame mobs.

Journalists, producers, actors, CEOS, television news anchors, comedians, onion writers, and pundits were called out or cancelled for offensive behaviors from the past or in the present.

However, in my view, the concept of calling someone out of social media will remain for some time to come. As long as people have a mobile phone to shoot video, a social media network to opine and hold a grudge, the cancel culture is a movement that leaders will need to navigate for the foreseeable future.

The good news is this culture, made up of people who think nothing of targeting people whom they deem as out of touch or on the wrong side of an issue, is not something to fear.

No, really!

Anyone can navigate this prickly culture by playing along with the rules followed by the people who inhabit it. Transparency and accountability are the secret rules to indestructibility.

A CULTURE OF CANDOR, A CALL FOR TRANSPARENCY

Until recently, organizations were largely allowed to operate within their own privacy guidelines set by their own leaders. Only reporters were allowed to ask questions, not the public at large. If the public did ask questions, their inquiries were dismissed, passed on to someone else, or ignored altogether.

If you were a company with a CEO who "never did interviews," members of the press abided by the rules and limited their questions to an assigned spokesperson. Boards of directors who met in executive sessions were allowed to bar outside members or visitors from the meetings, and people largely respected that.

"Transparency" became my buzzword in 2019. Every talk, every meeting with a client included the term and a call for adherence to the idea in their mindset and in their communications. Every so often, I would hear the reasons an organization couldn't share certain information with its constituents. The leaders of the organization or members of the board of directors would tell me a variety of excuses from "We don't have to share that information" to "If they want the information, they can find it themselves." Sometimes they said these things in a snarky way, but just as often it was delivered with earnest sincerity. They really did feel it wasn't anyone's business.

The people with whom I work are good people who care about their employees, consumers, and communities. They run reputable businesses and organizations and are well-respected in their communities. But they still cling to the outdated idea that everything is private unless they choose to release it.

Now, the game has changed. Modern-day consumers not only want information, they expect to receive it on demand. Being told "no" is an invitation to ask again and to ask even harder because the reluctance to share arouses suspicion.

Now that we are firmly set in a culture of sharing and receiving instant feedback through social media, people want instant information as well.

Transparency is a catchall word that says, "We're not hiding a thing." Just go ahead and let them in.

In my experience as a communications and public relations practitioner, I have witnessed every side of a leader's psyche—from the peak of their overconfidence to the depths of their vulnerability. Whether a CEO of a large company or owner of their own small business, these leaders inherently understand they are not only the face of the organization but also the visionary responsible for building a sustainable business and supporting its employees and the community it serves—not to mention just keeping the business afloat! Putting your vision, your experience out for everyone to see and judge can make anyone feel vulnerable.

True transparency takes more than just saying you are transparent; you have to show it and then share it. It's impossible to be a transparent leader, to run an organization with transparency, if you do not live it. And it affects all aspects of leadership.

Just the other morning I was giving a workshop to a roomful of communicators and member services representatives who work for electric cooperatives, the utilities that primarily make up the rural areas of the country. Cooperatives are a not-for-profit business model in which the members own the cooperative, so the needs of the members are paramount, unlike most private companies.

A few months earlier, I had submitted a proposal to a group of co-ops who were dealing with activist groups and an anti-co-op Facebook page. After submitting the proposal, I didn't hear a response. I followed up, but, again, heard nothing. It was more confusing than annoying—I knew this cooperative was committed to working on a solution.

Fast-forward to the conference, where I finally got my answer. The communicator who contacted me about working together on the project, informed me the CEO put the kibosh on my involvement due to something he heard me mention as an attendee in one of my talks or training sessions. I frequently mentioned I was a member of a Facebook group targeting a similar industry as this particular CEO's cooperative. My joining this group was a means for me to understand how these Facebook groups operated and to formulate strategies around how to manage it if one appeared in the service territory of a client. My participation was nothing more than a case study. This CEO looked at my membership as an act of treason.

It was the first time in my career as a consultant I had ever heard—and to my face no less—that someone did not want to hire me due to my communication practices. I did not look at that lost business as a repudiation of my work but rather a repudiation of his leadership. The excuse for not hiring me because I belonged to a Facebook group of concerned customers of my local utility was absurd in my opinion. The decision showed a lack of understanding for one of the most critical phases of a communication plan—the research. I dodged a bullet in my opinion, but any leader who was as close-minded as this one was bound to get hit at some point along the way.

Any leader who dismisses a Facebook group created for the purpose of questioning the policies and practices of their organization or business does so at their peril. These groups are powerful and are gaining more traction with Facebook's commitment to nurturing them for growth with their users.

In the past few years, Facebook in particular has pushed network-based, community-centered campaigns. The bad press and publicity from the election fallout (and the Cambridge Analytica issue) caused problems for the social network and Mark Zuckerberg's reputation. After testifying in front of Congress, Zuckerberg and his company needed to change the way they did business to better resonate with the public, the press, and Congress.

The push toward users' privacy was a good move and a necessary one to pacify the complaints against the social media network. To temper the critics, Facebook pivoted toward building online communities within the network and protecting people's privacy. To do this, they encouraged users to create groups, places where like-minded people can gather around common interests or beliefs. As I explained to the co-op CEOs and communicators, groups have power and shouldn't be ignored.

I spent four hours working with communicators on how to respond when a grassroot or activist group attacks a cooperative using primarily digital media. These are active groups with young, spirited, social media–savvy types that know how to share stories—and actively seek out stories to share.

It's up to you to listen to their stories.

CHAPTER 4

THE PRISON OF PUBLIC OPINION

In January 2020, Jennifer Aniston won The Screen Actors Guild Award for Outstanding Performance by a Female Actor in a Drama Series for her role as a morning news anchor in the Apple TV program *The Morning Show*. The limited series on the streaming network was on my radar, but the blip was well behind other television programs labeled under "Molly, have you watched blah blah? You'll love it!"

I was on the other side of *The Morning Show* buzz and could not believe this program got by me. Sheesh—after all, this is my business. My podcast episode on the downfall of Matt Lauer from his sexual and communications discretions was a favorite episode that practically wrote itself.

I knew Steve Carrell was cast in the program as a co-anchor to Jennifer Aniston's Alex Levy (who didn't scream news anchor, just sayin'), but the character of Mitch Kessler was directly lifted from Matt Lauer! How did I overlook this program?! And why did I not see coverage on the "'lift-from-the-headlines'" plot? I mean, after all, I am the target market for this type of program. Destroyed reputations via a viral mix of broadcast and social media is my bailiwick.

You may be thinking, *she actually thinks about this stuff?* Yes, I do . . . at least I did here.

The #MeToo movement still lingers and may never fully go away. I believe it's a fair assumption that most men will harbor fear their behavior could be called into question and discussed online. That's likely why Apple spent millions of dollars to produce the program *The Morning Show.*

"WHEN DID HUGGING BECOME A SIN?"

There's a wonderful scene in *The Morning Show* in which Martin Short's character discusses the incident behind the firing of Steve Carell's character. Short plays the role of director Dick Lundy, a director who has been similarly "cancelled" by the #MeToo movement. It's clear that Short's Lundy character is fictional, but his actions in the program are barely masked references to accusations made against directors Woody Allen and Roman Polanski. In episode 3 of the series, titled "Chaos Is the New Cocaine," the character of Lundy complains about fallout without addressing his own culpability, which he calls the shaming penalty a "prison of public opinion,"[4] and asked, "When did hugging become a sin?"

How true for anyone who has fallen on the wrong side of any movement.

Why are some people in the public eye sent away to prison of public opinion while others manage to break out?

THE SIGNS OF DESTRUCTIBILITY

As far as celebrities go, a cavalcade of people in the public eye, many of them men, have found themselves swept up in the #MeToo movement.

Some were able to manage their way out (just barely). Many have sought to rebuild or are in the process of rebuilding their reputations through some form of rehabilitation. But a few of the perpetrators found themselves in serious legal trouble from their behavior.

One celebrity who tipped the scales from inappropriate behavior to abhorrent and eventually landed himself in jail was America's (former) favorite dad, Bill Cosby.

---

4. *The Morning Show.* "Chaos Is the New Cocaine." 3. Directed by David Frankel. Written by Erica Lipez. Apple, Inc., November 1, 2019.

Up until the mid-2000s, Cosby appeared to have a bullet-proof reputation in public. Cosby was revered. His iconic television program *The Cosby Show* cemented his lovability as a husband and parent. Awards furthered his reputation along with commencement speeches, multiple honorary degrees, and meetings with moguls (Oprah) and presidents, along with a career-span of achievements.

It would take an event of seismic proportion to alter his reputation.

That event did happen in 2014, but it all began much earlier than that, in 2004. Cosby was convicted of drugging and molesting Andrea Constand, the former director of operations for the women's basketball team at Temple University in Philadelphia. That ruling opened the floodgates for multiple women to come forward and say Cosby assaulted them in the same fashion, some claims dating back to the 1960s. Although the times have changed greatly since then, Cosby's method of drugging and molesting women did not.

Few of these allegations stuck—at least until a comedian named Hannibal Buress called out Cosby during his standup routine.

The comedy set was captured on video, filmed by a person a number of rows back. The results are blurry; some parts are difficult to hear without replaying the video. But what *is* clear is his disbelief that Cosby chastises young black comedians who curse on stage—"Yeah, but you rape women, Bill Cosby, so turn the crazy down a couple notches."[5]

Buress adds his recommendation that the audience "Google 'Bill Cosby rape'" when they get home. He joked there would be a lot more results for that than a search for Hannibal Buress.

Hannibal Buress is often credited as the person who thrust the Bill Cosby story back into the spotlight, thus reigniting the calls to bring Cosby down. That credit is only partially true. If a comedian accuses a beloved comedian of rape in the woods, did it actually happen?

Buress started the ball rolling by mentioning Cosby in his set, but it was the video of that set going viral that created the momentum that landed Cosby behind bars.

---

5. McQuade, Dan. "Hannibal Buress on Bill Cosby: 'You're a Rapist.'" *Philadelphia*, October 17, 2014. https://www.phillymag.com/things-to-do/2014/10/17/hannibal-buress-bill-cosby-rapist/

How did that video bring down Bill Cosby? It touched the masses. Only a theater-full of people heard Buress rant about Cosby—people consisting of Buress fans and then-*Philadelphia Magazine* reporter Dan McQuade, who captured the set on his cell phone. Buress created the moment by mentioning it, but it was the reporter who decided to start filming when he heard Buress tread into Cosby territory. McQuade's news sense told him that he had a story on his mobile phone, and he was right.

Once the video went viral, the languishing stories about the Cosby allegations suddenly found footing, and more women felt compelled to speak it. The video opened the doors to conversations about Cosby's past and created a safe space for the women victimized by Cosby to come forward. The shift in public opinion against Bill Cosby protected those women and eventually brought Cosby down.

STEPS TO SELF-DESTRUCTIBILITY

Oftentimes when people complain to me about the impact of the #MeToo movement and how unfair it is or how out of hand it has become, I notice a catch in the voice that signals it's something else. These lamenters are mostly men in the fifty-plus age bracket. They shake their heads as they note the power of public opinion and what it can do to someone who is probably a decent person. It all seems so unfair to them. Of course, they are quick to admit, the people (men) who commit crimes or who are truly deviant in their behavior toward others (women) should be brought down.

I've spoken to enough of these guys to know what the real fear is. It's the arbitrary nature of the takedown that has them nervous. Could it happen to me? Could there be a person (woman) out there with a grudge or who wants financial gain from something I unconsciously or consciously did years ago during my ascension in the workplace?

If you have that fear, there is nothing I can write here to quell it. But I will state that the peak of the movement has passed, and if there was truly egregious behavior out there, there's a good chance it would have surfaced by now. That doesn't mean you're out of the woods, however; the #MeToo movement has opened the door for people who experienced some form of victimization. And in this social media age, this also means the door is open for the public to cast its judgment as well.

HOW CAN SOMEONE TELL IF THEIR "TIME IS UP"?

Although it may seem like people get cancelled suddenly and that they have no control over the situation, the reality is that those people do have some control. But they usually end up sabotaging themselves, making choices, decisions, and acts that cause these self-destructing events to happen. An off-the-cuff soundbite hits social media or a pre-planned statement released to the press or social media is so tone-deaf it lands with a thud that everyone can hear.

I speak not of the acts of a moral or legal nature; I'll let the moral police and people in law speak to that. I look at the moment in their communications when the person creates a trigger point, where their decision to act becomes painful.

That trigger point often comes from the influence of a crisis team (money is involved—lots of it) and well-intentioned advisors, friends, and family.

In the case of Bill Cosby, yes, he was in a legal morass: plenty of accusations but no charges yet. His reputation was taking plenty of hits, but he—and likely his team—felt they needed to right the ship.

Pro Tip: Most self-destructive moves typically happen when bad press meets impulsivity: "I have to do something *now!*" That something is usually an impulsive and costly move that triggers the start of the public downfall.

Bill Cosby's self-destructive moves were two decisions likely made to course-correct his reputation:

1. Donating over sixty works of African American art from Cosby's private collection for display at the Smithsonian National Museum of African American History and Culture.
2. Creating a "meme generator" contest to coincide with the launch of his updated program on Netflix.

The choices were clearly set out as diversionary tactics to reach Cosby's base of fans, which in itself was a cunning move. But they made a few critical miscalculations.

First, the donation.

No doubt the motivation behind the donation of a vast collection of African American art was three-fold:

1. Partnering with the esteemed Smithsonian Institution to remind people of Cosby's elevated status.
2. Donating a magnitude of work from his personal art collection to show extreme generosity.
3. Donating African American art to connect to the African American fan base.

In normal times, this would have been not only an appropriate PR move but a laudatory one. It combines good publicity with reminders of Cosby's immense wealth and influence. However, to make the donation and then publicize it during a period of bad press opens the door to further scrutiny. It's like leaving breadcrumbs to the next bombshell. In the case of the donation, the Associated Press later revealed that the Smithsonian concealed the fact that Bill and Camille Cosby had also funded a separate exhibition of African American artwork with a $716,000 donation that virtually covered the entire cost. Now that intense public scrutiny is part of our collective zeitgeist, a donation of this magnitude and nature seems like nothing more than a benevolent diversionary tactic to distract everyone from Cosby's troublesome reputation.

Smithsonian was faced with a "devil and the deep, blue sea" situation. The nautical phase is an idiom for a difficult choice. Should they have turned down a significant donation? Or should they have taken the money and hoped the public doesn't connect the museum with the accused rapist?

The Smithsonian chose poorly. The point when some other entity or person gets involved is a point when it's "'every man for himself'" and the scurry to protect reputations begins in earnest—a trigger point.

Second, the meme generator.

No one knows for certain how much of Bill Cosby's fan base is on social media, but knowing that his fame from comedy and television peaked in the late 1980s—which puts the bulk of the members in the forty-plus age bracket—it's safe to assume that social media isn't the best primary tactic for reaching the fans. Not a well-thought-out tactic for turning the momentum of the awful press.

What the team wanted was something like this:

However, what the team got was more along the lines of this:

Not surprising, the meme generator section of the Bill Cosby website (yes, he still has an active website) now displays this:

At the time of this PR launch, memes were catching on in the social crowd—the demographic of people comfortable interacting on social media. This was not the Bill Cosby base. Most of his fans have likely never even heard the term "meme," much less know how to create one, use one, or search for one on his website.

Creating a meme generator to reframe an accused sexual predator was so ill-advised it makes you wonder if it was an act of sabotage.

LESSON FOR LEADERS: WATCH FOR TRIGGER POINTS

Odds are, what happened to Bill Cosby will not happen to you—unless you're a popular public figure with a history of drugging and then molesting women or some other extreme moral failure. The valuable lesson of this story is in the response. Look at the trigger points of the Cosby story for lessons on how *not* to manage a crisis.

1. You are not bigger than anyone else.
2. Arrogance can blind you from a reasonable and common sense response.
3. Don't assume a story will "go away."
4. Don't play your crisis PR response in an area you're not familiar with.
5. Know the audience you need to sway.
6. Know your fan base and how to reach them.

The trigger tactics are usually well-intentioned but often not well-thought-out and executed without consideration of the current online climate. Crisis teams led by PR types who achieved some success pre-internet sometimes offer antiquated advice.

The team you use and the playbook everyone is working from should be managed for an age of digital and social media.

There are many PR-types and communicators who make a significant amount of money writing plans and providing toolkits to help manage a crisis. I am one of them. But I am also upfront about the practice, noting that many of them are worthless because they were written before viral media was an issue or do not include responses for online upsets.

THE OLD PLAYBOOK DOESN'T CUT IT ANYMORE

By this point you may be asking yourself, what do Bill Cosby and Matt Lauer have to do with me, a business owner or CEO?

Plenty.

Crises don't only happen to celebrities or well-known people; they happen to anyone in the business of having business with other people.

School superintendent.

Police chief.

Owner of the most popular restaurant in town.

CEO of a cooperative.

Dentist.

No one with any form of public profile is immune to a public cancelation influenced by social media. For the day-to-day working audience, take your lessons from people in the public eye.

In crisis management, there is a term called the "unknown unknowns." These are the events that no one can predict, nor prepare to handle, events that are so rare they can't be anticipated (though are often catastrophic). Nassim Nicholas Taleb, a finance professor and former Wall Street trader, calls these Black Swan events—situations that upend every response and business continuation plan and throw it into chaos.

Think 9/11.

Think COVID-19.

The impact of these Black Swan events is so significant because they reveal the vulnerabilities in many companies', agencies', and organizations' plans. When they happen, many are caught writing crisis and continuity plans for the first time rather than updating them.

Many crisis management professionals want their clients to treat viral media as an "unknown" and plan accordingly. However, in many cases, the impact of a social media blowback—or the threat of it—is dismissed by those clients.

Many leaders view social media as a communication channel filled with anonymous naysayers hiding behind an online alias or mobs of people online with nothing better to do than complain about successful people and businesses that are operating just fine, *thank you very much*. Anyone who dares complain or point out a flaw in a customer experience . . . well, they're solely out to bring us down for the count—and they're probably Millennials. (It's always the Millennials who get blamed for these things.)

Oftentimes, the leaders were the ones moving and shaking back in the time when a simple phone call to a journalist could fix a reputation ding. For bigger messes that needed to get cleaned up, a fixer was called in to handle the job.

The "old playbook" looks something like this:

Strategy: "Get me (or this business) out of this mess immediately!"

The head of public relations or communications got to work.

1. They made a phone call, and then held an interview with a journalist.
   - Big fish went to Barbara Walters or Diane Sawyer.
   - Not-so-big-fish went to the local beat newspaper reporter.
2. A press release or media statement was drafted, and an embargo was strategically lifted for one media outlet.
3. A genuine act of repentance was conceived (or concocted) to further an appearance of goodwill.

The old playbook was not heavy on accepting their role or—God forbid—an apology. No, the statement was always written in parsed language that didn't show a modicum of acknowledgment but used every euphemism for an apology without actually saying one. Apologies are an admission of guilt, so there was no need to acknowledge fault if they got a good story in the newspaper. Because in a time before the internet, the news was stale after twenty-four hours and was used to wrap fish.

Interview finished. Broadcast on national news or published in the newspaper—case closed.

Leaders today have updated the playbook—to a point. They may no longer rely so heavily on journalists or press releases, but many still go to any lengths to avoid accountability or apologies. This strategy doesn't fly with today's cancel culture.

LET'S STOP HERE FOR A MOMENT AND ASSESS

The goal of crisis management is to stop a crisis and lessen the damage impact. When crisis response uses denials and dismissals in the language, it can cause a crisis even greater than the one at hand. And *that's* how people get cancelled.

So how on earth do you, as a leader, navigate this startlingly different world of public opinion? For one thing, you have to be willing to leave the old playbook behind. And for another, you definitely have to change the way you think about technology.

CHAPTER 5

DIGITAL MISFITS AND DIGITAL NATURALS

You are a leader of an organization—a successful leader at that—but you sense your relevance is slipping. It's just a feeling. No one has come into your office, told you that you are trending downward, and instructed you to pack up and leave. But it strikes you that other people are getting ahead—or at least getting attention that you're not receiving.

You're not necessarily sinking, but others are ascending. There's some new, alternative digital world that they're mastering that seems foreign to you. Your communication tools consist of phone numbers in an address book—landline numbers that were updated with Post-It Notes, and then replaced with email addresses and mobile numbers. You know that you should transfer the valid information to a computer, and you'll do so someday. Yet you realize that even when that day comes, you'll have no idea how to do it.

You feel stuck.

It's a common situation. Getting unstuck requires getting past a mental block. The block that keeps you from transferring phone numbers from a physical address book to your smartphone is much like the one that's keeping you from understanding how to put yourself out there in this unfamiliar digital world that others seem to have mastered. The consequences of the phone-number block are minor—it's just harder to find information about someone you met at a convention three years ago. But the block that's keeping you from entering the larger digital sphere, the one in which your peers are getting ahead? That's holding you back professionally.

Admitting that you have the block is the first step. Tackling it is the next.

DIGITAL MISFITS

If you purchased this book and are now reading this paragraph, then you are likely a Digital Misfit.

Welcome.

The fact that you reached this point in the journey tells me a lot about you already. You know you need to learn more about technology and digital media, but even more important—you want to. Or at the very least, you know you need to learn it to be a truly effective leader in the modern age.

How do I know this? Because this group is more likely to choose a book to learn. It's comforting to crack open a book and touch the pages, to take in the smell of printed ink. It's not only the sensory aspect that draws you in but the independent learning that takes place. You're reading the book by yourself. Until you recommend it or talk about it in a book club, the experience is yours alone until you decide to share it. You can learn how to become more relevant in the social game with no one looking over your shoulder.

Now, why the label of a Digital Misfit? The term misfit means someone who is unable to adapt to their circumstances. Sound familiar? When I think of the word misfit, my mind immediately goes to an island off the North Pole. A lot of the Baby Boomers and Gen Xers may remember Rudolph the Red-Nosed Reindeer visiting the Island of Misfit Toys with his friend Hermey ("I want to be a dentist!") and Yukon Cornelius. The inhabitants on the Island of Misfit Toys are a collection of unloved or unwanted toys (misfits) who were brought to the island by a winged lion called King Moonracer. He gives them a home on the island until he can place them with children who will love them and accept them. The person who doesn't know why anyone would use Twitter could be the water gun that squirts jelly. The person who doesn't know how to caption a post they shared on Facebook is like Charlie-in-the-Box. Can't tweet your way around Twitter? You feel like the cowboy who rides an ostrich.

No one wants to feel like a misfit, but it is inevitable if your livelihood is starting to depend on your participation in the online space. But take solace in the fact that the difference between a Digital Natural and a Digital Misfit is a thinner line than you may realize, and it doesn't take years of computer learning to change.

Here is an important point to consider: being a misfit is not a critique. I use this term not to diminish or mock a person's digital acumen, but to quell anxiety over the lack of knowledge. It's okay to not have a handle on all forms of technology. I don't.

I can tweet with the best of them but watch me try to navigate Snapchat or sync my headphones on my iPhone—misfit.

Not sure if you're a Digital Misfit or a Digital Natural? See if any of this sounds familiar to you.

It was only a few years ago that you didn't feel any pressure to be on Facebook. You never understood why anyone would want to waste so much time on the platform sharing *everything* about themselves. But then you slowly start to notice how people seem to know more information about your friends and family than you do. They are sharing conversations, but you wonder how often everyone is meeting without you. *Why isn't anyone inviting me into these conversations?* You feel left out. But soon enough you realize because people are talking about conversations that happened on Facebook and not in person. You have to swap one disappointment for another.

You aren't entirely sure what the conversation is, but you are acutely aware you're missing it. The bottom line is that the people who are using social media are more in the know than you. You still think it all may be a huge waste of time, but you know you can't fight it any longer. But where to begin? What profile to create? And when you do, what would you say? Do you have anything to say or share that anyone even cares about?

Why does it matter?

It matters because you understand it is never going to change. The world will not go back to primarily communicating face-to-face. We all live in a digital society now, and for those of us not on social media, it's our own fault if we're missing out.

It's not just the personal conversations and the sharing of photos; you feel that the whole world is moving online. Your friends are on Facebook, your clients are on Twitter, and your colleagues and other people in your industry on LinkedIn.

Rest assured, there are far more Digital Misfits out there than the nineteen toys on the island. Most Baby Boomers, Traditionalists, and a number of Generation Xers were Digital Misfits at one time. The only way to shake the label is to dig in and learn how to use it.

Simply put, a Digital Natural is someone who is comfortable using technology.

Full stop.

That's it. The book in a nutshell. The secret sauce.

DIGITAL NATURALS

In order to understand how to navigate this online world of digital technology and social media, you must one, understand that it exists, and two, understand that it should be incorporated into your professional strategy if you want to maintain your relevancy and to succeed in your professional world.

A Digital Natural is someone who feels comfortable with a smartphone in their hands. They are not afraid of the technology but are acutely aware of the risk of oversharing or not pausing before hitting send.

This person may sound like a Millennial or a teenager, but that is not necessarily the case. Digital Naturals are not a particular age or a member of a particular generation. That's too limiting. Being a Digital Natural is only a way of thinking. If you want to be comfortable in the technology space, all you need to do is learn the tips for using technology only in the areas you want to. It's not an-all-or-none proposition.

Yes, many Digital Naturals reside on college campuses and are on the sidelines of high school football games. They are the moms taking photos of their children at the playground with their phone, and teenagers who have streaks on Snapchat. But Digital Naturals are also fifty-five-year-old men who like to keep track of the miles they biked on the weekend with a fitness app and the members of a retirement community who all belong to the same cooking Facebook group to share their recipes and plan meetings. A Digital Natural is someone who is naturally curious about how technology can make their lives easier and is not afraid to try and learn the technology. They do have a healthy amount of fear, but the fear does not manifest itself as paralysis but rather as a drive to learn.

No one wants to feel like a misfit, but it is inevitable if your livelihood is starting to depend on your participation in the online space. Why do you need to become a Digital Natural? It's not a difficult question to answer. It's simple—*Why not?*

A tad flippant, I know, but it sums up the answer rather succinctly. I have yet to hear of a compelling reason from anyone as to why they shouldn't get on board with using technology or digital media to help improve their communications. I suspect the answer lies in the ideology rather than the work itself. People don't like to be told how they need to behave, but there's also a fear of the unknown—"I would be open to learning about digital media, but I have absolutely no idea what I am doing and I am afraid to ask anyone for fear of looking stupid or, worse, out of touch."

The good news is that the key to adapting to this technology is not a how-to, it's only shifting your mindset. That's it.

The problems lie in the interpretation of the questions. People who are reluctant to join the digital world think they need to dig in and change how they use technology. Not so. A Digital Natural is only someone who accepts that technology is here and is open to using it to help them in their professional and personal life.

But I guess staying a Digital Misfit is fine if:

- You want to live off-the-grid.
- You don't want to be bothered by people online.
- You don't want to waste time on digital media and technology.
- You want to be left alone.
- You take pride in your anachronic way of thinking.

If any of those reasons resonate with you, then, by all means, stay where you are. And I don't mean that remark to sound snarky in any way.

There are plenty of people who do not want to be bothered or found anywhere else unless the person is standing right in front of them.

But being a Digital Natural is definitely worth it if you:

- Run a business or brand.
- Have family and friends that you want to stay in touch with on a (semi-) regular basis.
- Want to succeed at your job.
- Want the benefit of networking without having to leave your office.
- Want to learn.
- Want to connect.
- Want to succeed.
- Want to stay up to date on the news and your interests.

There are too many reasons to list here, but you get the idea. The world is communicating online. Business, sports, personal interactions—they're *all* happening online. If you want to be in the mix, you have to be willing to shed the misfit.

Digital Natural. No one will know, like, or trust you if you are not comfortable working, living and breathing in the same space where the public resides—online.

I'll let you in on a secret: Everyone has a struggle with social media and technology in some form or another. It all depends on when it was introduced in a person's school years or professional years.

Millennials, with the introduction of technology at some point in their education, are technically savvy in many areas. They are wired to be good at using technology and having it at their fingertips. Following closely behind are the kids in Generation Z. They are even more wired in, but they also have a strong psychological connection to their devices. How many likes on Instagram or how long of a streak on Snapchat are important metrics in their lives. However, these same savvy "bulletproof" millennials don't spend much time worrying about oversharing information on their personal life, how they feel about a boss, or using inappropriate language. It seems as if they forget "the internet is forever."

At the other end of the spectrum are the Traditionalists and the Baby Boomers who definitely did not have any technology in the schoolroom. I'm talking chalk on a chalkboard and pencils on paper.

Generation X had technology likely introduced in the later years of their education. Most, if not all, started their schooling without any technology. Writing utensils were the tools for learning. Computers were introduced late in middle school or college for the older members of Gen X. This hybrid generation's first glimpse of technology was likely a projector.

Traditionalists: You may struggle with adding an email to your phone, but I bet you have amazing penmanship.

Baby Boomers: You don't know how to start a group on Facebook, but you can probably type 200 words a minute.

Generation Xers: You can't understand how to set up a geotag on Snapchat, but you are pretty good at basic HTML.

Just because you're not a Millennial doesn't mean that there's no hope for you! In fact, each generation has its own set of valuable skills and experiences. Becoming a Digital Natural is not about trading one set of skills for another but about developing both to build off each other.

EXAMPLES OF DIGITAL MISFITS

Senator Dianne Feinstein

Backstory: Senator Feinstein literally walked into her "Misfit" status when she found herself in a standoff with a group of schoolchildren accompanied by people with cell phones. Her moment came on the heels of the Green New Deal, proposed by the Queen of the Congressional Call Out, Alexandria Ocasio-Cortez. At the time of the event, one could argue that Ocasio-Cortez was reaching a zenith in popularity. The Green New Deal was a very ambitious environmental proposal that called for the public to buy into a future without airplanes or carbon footprints. As a first-year congresswomen, Ocasio-Cortez almost seemed to revel in making her older colleagues look out of touch. Many, if not all, seemed to take the bait.

Ocasio-Cortez wasn't anywhere even close to the action in the hallway, but her influence was felt when the kids started to pepper Senator Feinstein with questions. Appalled by the kids' boldness, Feinstein dodged and weaved their questions.

And these kids were no slouches—they were a group of a congressional press corps in the making. Each one followed a well-articulated question with another question. Each addressed the senator with respect and asked pressing questions on the referendum. This particular group was almost too good. I'd bet my money that these kiddos went a round or two with an activist-minded coach or parent. Senator Feinstein likely had no idea she was walking into an orchestrated event.

Feinstein tried to explain her side, detailing why Ocasio-Cortez's proposal would not work in the current political climate. But instead of coming off as the gentle schoolteacher, gracefully explaining her opposition to the Green New Deal, the prickly Feinstein began to lose her patience and started to lecture the youngsters about why she opposed the Green New Deal. Her mistake was looking down and being drawn into the multitude of questions being lobbed at her. For had she looked up, she would have noticed the phones trained on her, recording the whole thing.

The video was eventually posted by the Sunrise Movement, an organization that encourages young people to combat climate change (and long-serving senators apparently). The incident proved to be a tidy little press op for the group, since the story of the hallway interaction went viral.

In her defense, the tactic used against Senator Feinstein is a common one for activists to try and create an artificial viral moment. However, posting an awkward viral moment will grab more eyeballs than describing the method to achieve it.

How can you spot the move of a Misfit? When an event unravels in the public space, there is a strong likelihood that it will be filmed and end up popping up somewhere online. When that event includes Millennials, Generation Z kids, and likely their parents, it's almost guaranteed to end up online. Senator Feinstein was more focused on convincing a group of kids that she was right rather than noticing that she was a part of a click-worthy video in the making.

The Context: Senator Feinstein stumbled into an event that more or less exploited her Misfit status. The interaction in the hallway smacked of a set-up, and many people would have reacted the same way. There is no shame in not knowing to look up for a phone filming an event. Perhaps if a television appeared in Feinstein's line of sight, she would have reeled in the lecture.

The Takeaway: Public events rarely happen in a vacuum. If you are the center of attention, or close to it, you are likely being photographed or filmed. Go into every situation knowing you could be filmed.

Kevin Spacey, Actor

Backstory: Kevin Spacey was dropped from his Netflix show *House of Cards* and replaced in the film *All the Money in the World* after he was accused of forcing himself on a minor (now an adult), actor Anthony Rapp. He apologized through a statement on Twitter. Since then, more men have come forward accusing Mr. Spacey of behaving inappropriately toward them.

Trigger: In a tweet responding to the allegations, Spacey dodged the accusation by using the passage of time and the haze of intoxication to explain his alleged behavior that he claimed not to remember. In paragraph two of the statement, he chose to address his sexuality and come out as a gay man. Gay men, and the rest of the population it seemed, were not having it.

Addressing sexual transgressions on a minor via tweet is wrong.

"This story encouraged me to address other things about my life. . . . As those closest to me know, in my life, I have had relationships with both men and women. I have loved and had romantic relationships with men throughout my life, and I choose now to live as a gay man."[6]

Not the time, not the medium. Since that 2017 tweet, Spacey has essentially been embroiled in controversy after controversy. Several allegations of sexual assault appeared along with a leaked photo of Spacey with Ghislaine Maxwell (the woman at the center of the Jeffrey Epstein

---

6. Spacey, Kevin. Twitter Post. October 29, 2017, 10:00 p.m. https://twitter .com/KevinSpacey/status/924848412842971136.

scandal) at Buckingham Palace when they were guests of another scandal-plagued party, Prince Andrew, the Duke of York.

WHEN DIGITAL MISFITS AND DIGITAL NATURALS COLLIDE

Jennifer Willoughby is a Digital Natural.

If you don't recognize the name, you may remember the story of her former husband, Rob Porter. In 2017, Porter, the White House staff secretary, was working for President Trump when his personal life collided with his public one: it was discovered that he was accused of domestic abuse from both of his former wives.

According to press reports, Porter's first wife, Colbie Holderness, said she had been physically abused multiple times throughout her marriage to Porter. They divorced in 2008. In 2009, Porter married Willoughby. After repeated abuse, she obtained a restraining order against him, and they divorced in 2013.

What happened next, however, was the trigger point that eventually caused Rob Porter to lose his job at the White House. It came from the hands of Porter's second wife, Jennifer Willoughby, by way of a blog.

I spoke with Willoughby, who goes by Jennie, for my podcast about her story illustrating how viral media can start a crisis. Willoughby is bright, kind, and compassionate. Not a vindictive bone in her body. Her cause is to help people, women especially, who have suffered abuse, anger, stress, or trauma, and she helps through mindfulness and transforming their narratives that brought them there.

Willoughby wrote a blog post that went viral, detailing the abuse she suffered at the hands of Porter that launched a national scandal and eventually sparked the global hashtag #AndSoIStayed.

The hashtag led people, most notably reporters, to the door of the White House. In a time when the #MeToo movement was starting to gain steam, it was a reasonable question to ask if an abuser was working in the White House.

In my opinion, the Rob Porter story blew up because an employee of a Digital Natural president had a chief of staff who was by all indications a Digital Misfit.

The esteemed General Kelly was a decorated soldier with a proven track record to lead. He had the hardware and the field experience to show for it. However, for all that strategic military experience, the general may have had another label that clouded his decision-making choices as it related to Rob Porter—Digital Misfit. I assume that, in the fog of the war against Rob Porter, General Kelly knew about the blog post by Jennifer Willoughby but dismissed it.

I pictured him being briefed in his office, distracted by other news, and telling someone, "It will go away. No one is going to read something online written by a woman no one knows or cares about." Mind you, that's my interpretation of events. I could be way off. But I asked Jennie Willoughby if I was. I suspected she felt the same as me.

Turns out she did feel the same. Word got back to her that the White House, most notably General Kelly, did dismiss her and her blog with the hopes it would go away. The fact he wanted to keep Rob Porter on staff pretty much confirmed it.

However, Jennie Willoughby and her blog did not go away. It went viral along with her hashtag and can be argued as the reason Rob Porter no longer officially works at the White House. No one can be certain that he hasn't been hired for ad hoc work in support of President Trump, but from an optics and public relations point of view, the White House—and by extension President Trump—would be excoriated if they hired a spousal abuser back.

Jennie Willoughby's blog made certain of that fact.

Meanwhile, Jennifer Willoughby is a successful speaker focusing on grace and redemption. She is now specializing in speaking and helping people understand the **Cancel Culture and the road to forgiveness and redemption.**

Digital Naturals: 2
Digital Misfit: 0

IT'S ALL IN THE ROUTINE

At this point, you are either warming up to the description of the Digital Misfit or a little put off—or both. And that's okay. I want to stress here that being a Digital Misfit is not a bad thing. There's no shame in not knowing how to use every piece of technology. It's okay to admit you may be a Misfit. And if you're unsure if you really are a Misfit—well, you're still reading this book, right?

Being a Misfit isn't about how others perceive you but how you perceive yourself. I recognize this feeling in other people so often I can almost smell it: embarrassment, shame, distrust for all things digital— I've seen it all.

It may be more helpful to define a Digital Misfit by explaining what it is not. The Misfit is not someone who does not know how to use an iPhone or how to use Apple AirDrop or know what an iOS system is.

The Misfit is a mindset. That's it. It's not a set of skills you don't have but a set of skills you refuse to acquire for a number of reasons. It's simply a marker indicating that there is room to shift your knowledge base from traditional to digital. This does *not* mean you have to abandon your traditional ways. In fact, quite the opposite. It's incredibly beneficial to keep up with the solid skills—the hard skills—that keep a person relevant in the modern age.

Writing, speaking, enjoying the feeling of a newspaper in one hand and a hot cup of coffee or tea (skim latte for me, please) in the morning— they all have a place in the digital world. Personally, having newsprint in my left hand with the heat of a beverage in my right seems to open my mind. My subconscious brain knows it's time to read and to take in information. My brain, no matter how tired or sluggish I am in the morning, is ready to read the front page. It allows me to go deep into a news story and retain the details from the photographs, quotes, and insight from the reporter. I can take in the Metro section, art and entertainment, real estate, and sports. I can scan box scores quickly and know exactly who is in what place. And finally, my brain is ready for the *Parade Magazine* (which is much smaller than it was from years ago but still the perfect way to top my Sunday paper reading). This Sunday morning routine, whether I am at home or in a hotel for work or a sports tournament with my kids, is the same every Sunday. And if I have the time, I squeeze the CBS Sunday Morning program to really get wired in on what is happening with the world. Ten years ago, I would have said Meet the Press with Tim Russert, but when he sadly left the program after his death in 2008, so did I.

If I start my week this way, then I know it's going to be a productive "firing on all cylinders" kind of a week. And if I get to a Saturday or Sunday Mass, then I know I am really going to have a heck of a week.

This Sunday routine is cemented into my life; it's been there for years and it has benefitted me for years. And without it, I would be spinning my wheels trying to keep up with all the information. If I relied on my phone or my laptop to consume the weekly news on a Sunday morning, I am confident I would miss most of it. My routine is so effective for me because it's organized: step-by-step, my brain takes in the content in layers, all timed perfectly. By comparison, the blitzkrieg of the internet news is overwhelming. It's fine when you are standing in line waiting to buy coffee, but not for sitting down at breakfast.

Just looking at the absence of technology in my Sunday morning routine, you might think I'm a Misfit myself. But I also strongly advocate, suggest, teach, and scream on the mountaintops (a.k.a. tweet it) to encourage people, especially leaders in business, to go all-in on digital. While my routine is traditional, my mindset is all about using digital and social media in my life to help me become more productive, more relevant, a more sought-after speaker . . . whatever I want to improve on. Once you accept the idea of technology, you can begin to introduce technologies and digital practices into your professional and personal world that will benefit you down the road.

Never ever—and this is critical to success—abandon your traditional ways of communicating or receiving communications. After all, we have to speak with each other. Communication is an absolutely essential skill. We're never going to abandon the spoken word, but there are many places where sending an email or sending a text is more efficient than seeking someone out to speak with them.

Let's say you want to set up a meeting to try and sell a product to a potential client. Are you going to leave your desk and head down to your car to drive across town to ask to meet in person? Of course not; a phone call or email can do the trick.

That's the idea of being a Digital Natural. Find the communication hacks in your life that will make your professional and personal life easier. Once you do, you will immediately see the benefits that are guaranteed to make you more relevant—or at least appear to be, and after all, isn't that the same thing? In other words, you'll be a modern-age communicator.

TIME CHECK

Let's go back a bit in time. Think of when you first heard about Facebook. It was likely sometime around the 2008 election. What were your initial thoughts about the social network?

Let me take a stab at it:

1. "Why are people wasting their time on such a stupid thing?"
2. "I don't get it."
3. "All I see people do is post items on Facebook that make them look stupid."
4. "Don't people have better things to do with their time?"

I've heard them all and more, long after 2008. I hear these objections now on a routine basis. But back then I remember hearing it almost exclusively from people fifty and older—specifically from my own mother and others in that pre-Baby Boomer generation crowd.

The path to accepting Facebook into your life is a lot like Elisabeth Kübler-Ross and David Kessler's Five Stages of Grief:

- Denial
- Anger
- Bargaining
- Depression
- Acceptance

Denial

- "What is Facebook and why do I even need to care about it?"
- "It's a fad and will go away soon."

- "Only kids use The Facebook. Once they grow up, they'll realize how much of a waste it is and it will go away."
- "I'm not on Facebook, so you'll have to send the kid's soccer schedule to me separately."

Anger

- "Why does our company have to get a Facebook Page?!"
- "I hate it when I try to talk to someone and all I see is their head buried in a phone."
- "Why does so-and-so post such stupid things to Facebook? Has she no shame?"
- "I don't know why you all would want to waste so much time on that thing!"

Bargaining

- "Okay, I'll get an account, but I'm going to share it with my wife."
- "Fine! I'll create an account, but I'm not going to use it."
- "Go ahead and make me one of the people in charge of the company Facebook Page, but don't expect me to post anything. I have more important things to do at work."

Depression

- "I feel like everyone is on Facebook except for me."
- "I hate being on Facebook, but if I'm not, I feel like I'm missing out on events."
- "It's seems like I am out of the loop if I don't check it every day."

Acceptance

- "Gah! Fine! I'll use it."

Not to make light of actual grief, of course, but there is a life-altering shift that happens when someone's routine changes. While the Kübler-Ross stages traditionally outline the journey of losing someone close to you, with social media the journey is the opposite—it's coming to accept being connected to so many people at once. Either one requires making a huge adjustment to your life.

Are you still with me? What I'm saying is that reluctance to accept social media is common. It's normal human behavior to resist change in your life, especially if it's tied into both your professional and personal life. And in this case, you're adjusting to not only how you use social media but how other people use it as well. Part of the reluctance toward and distrust of social media, I find, is that people feel forced to conform to how other people use it.

How you use technology is your own business. The Digital Misfit label is effectively removed once a person accepts their own limitations regarding technology. When a social media–challenged person asks for help when they need it, refrains from blaming the technology for the problem, and then takes the time to try and remember what they've learned—well, they're on their way to becoming a Digital Natural.

CHAPTER 6

BECOMING A DIGITAL NATURAL

I never have a straight answer when someone asks me what I do for work. To me, my job is as clear as day, of course, because I am at it each and every day. Okay, yes—sadly, as a solo entrepreneur, more often than not it is *every* single day (but that's okay in most cases because I love what I do).

The true elevator pitch about what I do is varied, so it's much easier to digest from a bio, but in short, my mission is this:

I help people deliver the right message at the right time on the right channel. My value system is the need for accountability in today's communications. I show leaders the power behind truth and transparency, especially in a time of crisis.

I help people become modern-age communicators in their industry and build crisis-resilient businesses. I am an APR-certified public relations practitioner who combines my knowledge of current social media tools and practices with my years of news and public relations experience.

If I were to talk about the goals I often hear from clients, it's not so clear. I hear countless questions like this:

- How can I get my boss to understand the importance of using social media in our business?
- Our association is getting pressure by our local senator about this issue, and we need a plan. What do we do?

- How do I get the directors on our board to understand that we need more money in the budget for our communications?
- How the heck do I create a LinkedIn profile?

These *asks* from people rarely have a set objective, as in, "We need to increase the views on the live feed of our annual meeting by twenty percent from year to year."

The goals are fuzzy and without many definitions. There is a need for "something" to happen, but the ask often lacks specifics because, I find, the person asking doesn't have a clue what they are really asking for.

It's difficult to assess whether the goals aren't realistic, or the people simply don't understand the connection between marketing and communication strategies and outcomes. Marketing is a piece of the communication plan, but most executives in my experience have no idea how much time and energy and patience go into it. So much of it is a slow burn.

I have been in business long enough to know that it usually comes down to the same feeling—fear.

Whatever that fear is, it creates a block.

- "How can I get my boss to understand the importance of our business using social media?" actually means "Can you convince my boss we need a Facebook page?"
- "Our association is getting pressure by our local senator about an issue and we need a plan. What do we do?" actually means "This story is already public and now I have a senator breathing down my neck. I will lose this job if you can't help me create a plan."
- "How do I get the directors on our board to understand we need more money in the budget for our communications?" actually means "Can you show this board of directors that if we do not have more money for resources, we won't be able to protect their reputation if they say something odd to the press?"
- "How the heck do I create a LinkedIn profile?" actually means "Can you create a LinkedIn profile for me, so I don't look out of touch?"

The fear is legitimate. People aren't comfortable with knowledge gaps, and with how quickly that gap can increase with the constant changes and updates in technology, it becomes disheartening. Many people are ashamed of how little they know about how apps and programs work, but the truth is, many people feel the same way. I don't believe even Mark Zuckerberg can keep up with all the changes and updates on his own network. I think it's fair to assume he knows more than most in his role running Facebook, but does he have the time to know everything? Not a chance.

How can someone remove the block and let go of the fear? Simple. Tell someone you need the help.

This simple strategy breaks through a lot of walls that are preventing people from learning how to use technology. If you're worried about looking stupid—don't. It's all in the framing. Don't tell people you are too old or too dumb to understand technology. Even worse, don't tell people it's a waste of time but you need to figure it out for work.

The key is to move your ego aside for a moment and simply ask for help. People love helping other people, especially with tasks that come easy to one but not necessarily the other.

The quickest way to get from Digital Misfit to Digital Natural is to ask someone how to do it.

Still not convinced that you could become a Digital Natural? Here's a story for you: Mike Carlton is a Marine Corps combat veteran in his early forties who served for five years in the US Marines. Mike started a moving and storage business after he transitioned out of the military. Mike was the former leader of a sniper team deployed to places like Kosovo and Albania, where he helped and protected refugees like women and children coming out of Kosovo.

Mike Carlton is a mix of gritty and compassionate—a perfect combination for a business leader. After his time in the service, he applied that gritty work ethic into building a "best in class" move and storage business called Calling All Cargo.

The company's mission: Moving with a purpose.

That mission statement could be Mike Carlton's statement for how he manages the operations and promotion of his business. Everything has a purpose.

His business was successful, and based on his website and social media efforts, you would have thought he was an early adopter of online promotion and advertising.

However, Mike admits he lacks expertise in digital marketing and feels as if he is far behind similar businesses. Mike would call himself a Digital Misfit, but he is solidly a Digital Natural—he just doesn't know it. Because what comes natural to Mike Carlton showed up in the social media efforts he was doing.

Mike didn't need to tell people he was hard-working and had a reliable moving staff because you could see that in the efforts he did on social media.

Mike is laser focused. It's no surprise he was a sniper in the military; once he knows he needs to fix something in his business, he researches what he needs to do and then goes for it.

This is the mark of a Digital Natural.

Mike is self-deprecating when he discusses his social media talent. He doesn't believe he has any. Yet, his business Facebook page is filled with the types of posts you would find in a social media "how to" guide. Mike admits to having a basic level of understanding when it comes to using social media for his business; however, the numbers of "likes," "followers," and views of his posts tell a different story. Mike's superpower, when it comes to his business's social media page, is his eagerness to learn. Not what he *knows* about social media, but what he's *learned*.

Remember that sentence if you own or operate a small business.

Mike is not an extroverted person, but he is overly passionate about his employees and his business, which means he is a natural for sharing the news about both on social media. Many people cringe at the thought of sharing a video clip of themselves online sharing news about their business. Not Mike. He has no reservations whatsoever creating and sharing videos to his Facebook followers about his impressive crews and the service they are providing for customers.

When Mike felt like he needed to reach a younger demographic for hiring, he suspected that Instagram would be a good place to start finding them. He was right. Photos and videos of his crews at work helped potential employees see for themselves how well Calling All Cargo treated its employees and crews.

Mike has been honored with the "Top 10 to Watch" award for young leaders in the seacoast area of Maine and New Hampshire, along with the Dover and the BBB Torch and Perfect Record awards. When he received an award, Mike would share the news on social media—but not in a self-aggrandizing way. When Calling All Cargo won the 2020 Dover, N.H., Chamber of Commerce Business of the Year award, Mike didn't talk about himself; he thanked everyone for helping him.

When the coronavirus outbreak hit New England, Mike was ready. Moving companies were considered an essential business, so Mike made sure he took care of his employees first and then gave frequent updates on social media to all key stakeholders: his customers—current and potential—and his employees and crew. He shared valuable and verified information from the federal and state government officials. He shared information learned from operating his small business during a pandemic to help any small business owner navigate in this time of uncertainty.

Mike Carlton is the George Bailey of the moving and storage business. Instead of running the Bailey Brothers' Building and Loan to serve the fictitious community of Bedford Falls, Calling All Cargo serves its employees and customers first before the owner.

How does everyone know it? Not because Mike Carlton tells people he runs his business that way; it's because he shows it numerous times a week on social media.

That is the true tell of Digital Natural. The leader who is confident in their natural abilities to share is digitally.

GUESS WHAT? YOU'RE ALREADY A NATURAL.

Yes, you read that correctly. You are likely already a Digital Natural in many aspects. All you need to do now is find, like Mike did, where your talents match up with the needs of your profession.

The first step is to figure out where your natural abilities lie. What are you naturally good at in terms of soft and hard skills?

Identify what you are naturally good at or known for. Where is your safe place in your line of work? Look at the combination of hard skills and soft skills that make you a business success in the face-to-face world.

- Are you a good writer?
- Are you a good salesperson?
- Do you love to network?

- Does speaking to people on stage come easy to you?
- Are you the type of person who has no problem walking into a room alone and introducing yourself to people?
- Are you great with numbers?

All these talents and skills can easily transfer into the digital realm even if you don't think you have the aptitude for it. Let's break down the skills I listed above.

Are you a good writer?

If you write a weekly column for the company newsletter, take the same article, make a few changes, and publish it on LinkedIn to share with your network. Or write a letter from the CEO (general manager, head of safety, head of accounting, etc.) and publish it online. In other words, if you love to write or consider yourself to be more eloquent with the written word rather than the spoken word, then write! Blogging, posting on social media, and heck, even commenting on social media, are all forms of writing

Are you a good salesperson?

If you're comfortable selling the product and, by extension, yourself to other people to make the sales, you're a perfect fit for social media. A natural salesperson is usually considered valuable because they aren't selling a product; instead, they are selling a solution to a problem. Design an email to be sent out to clients or potential customers, and instead place of writing out your sales pitch, have a video of the natural salesperson explaining the benefits of the business or the product. Videos are the key driver to engagement online, so let that natural salesperson shine online.

Do you love to network?

If the answer is yes, then you are likely already on LinkedIn. Believe it or not, this business platform isn't much different from Facebook. It's a place for people to connect online for the purpose of networking. Sharing your knowledge and connecting with people are natural leads to a sale. Reach out to people who can get you one step (or one click) closer to a key decision maker at a company. LinkedIn is one big cocktail party or pre-conference meetup without the travel. The growth of LinkedIn in recent years proves how effective it can be in helping users grow their networks.

Does speaking to people on stage come easy to you?

Oh, this one is easy. The very people who light up the stage are the same type of people who can light up a social media post. If you do well in a social environment, you're probably the type of person who can bring the same charisma to a video shared online. Do you have a prepackaged sales pitch or a talk you give frequently in a professional setting? Put it on film the next time you give it, then share it on social media. If it's longer than three minutes, cut it up in a series of talks and drip the content.

Are you the type of person who has no problem walking into a room alone and introducing yourself to people?

If you don't have any problem meeting people, then it's likely you will not have any trouble reaching out to people online. Friend someone on Facebook. Follow someone on Twitter, then send them a DM to further connect with them. Reach out to someone you do not know on LinkedIn but who's in the same field of work as you. Creating a mutually beneficial relationship with someone you may never meet but could turn into a wildly successful online relationship. Or connect two people you know on LinkedIn together. Tell them why they should connect and where the benefit lies.

Do you have a knack for numbers?

Okay, I'm throwing this skill into the mix because it has absolutely nothing to do with social media—not a skill easily transferable to the digital world. Could a numbers person be a Digital Natural? Sure. If you are an analytical type, then that may mean you like to follow the numbers to reach a conclusion. Go behind the numbers on one social media site or take a crack at all of them at the same time. Establish where you are now for a baseline and then see how much you grow. Track your personal analytics on your social media sites. How many friends have you gained in the past year? How often do you engage on Facebook? How many connections do you have on LinkedIn? What was your growth in the past year? Share a post on LinkedIn, and then see how many people engage with that post. LinkedIn has an excellent analytical tool for shared posts. After a few people engage (like or comment) you will eventually have access to the detailed analytics. You'll see where the people work and live and their job title. Analytics are fun to watch, but the real benefit comes from watching the growth. Where did it come from and how can you build on it? Check out the impressions on Twitter from a tweet. It's almost immediate. By looking at the impressions and the time of day, you'll learn the best time of day to tweet. There are programs out there that will do it for you, but if you are a numbers person, perhaps the fun is in figuring it out yourself.

Whatever your skills are, the key to becoming a Digital Natural is starting well within your comfort zone. It doesn't matter which social network you start off with to get your feet wet; choose the one you consider the safest at the moment. Some people might start with LinkedIn because people tend to only publish and comment on professional matters. But maybe your profile isn't up to snuff yet and you want to hold off until it's ready.

You could start on Twitter because it moves so quickly, and people may not even notice you are on the site before you start tweeting. You could open an account—and do use your name—but don't follow anyone you know at first. Follow the accounts that interest you. It could be a local newspaper, a sports team, or a famous writer. Most people in the professional limelight have a Twitter account. Look for the blue verified check—that means it's a real account. However, when you do decide to jump in and tweet, be careful what you post; many politicians, athletes, and other leaders have come under fire in recent years when their old, insensitive tweets came to light. Start clean from the get-go.

Facebook and Instagram are difficult to use under the radar because they are connected together so tightly (Facebook owns Instagram). Once you open an account and start to fill in the profile, artificial intelligence takes over and starts to find "friends" for you based on your real connections. All it takes is one friend and one person following you and AI does the rest. People who likely know you in real life will get notifications that you are now on social media and you should be friends or follow each other.

Both Facebook and Instagram are fairly safe places to play; Instagram is much easier because it is driven primarily by images. As long as you're not posting risqué photos or videos, you'll be fine.

The lesson is this: start simple. Jump into social media on the platform you feel most comfortable and start following along. When you start to follow the ebb and flow, jump in and see how it goes. I think you'll find it's okay and maybe a little addicting once you get going.

The next step is to showcase your skills. Remember, if you are a natural writer, then see if your company will publish your column on a company website or on LinkedIn or start commenting on other people's pieces. Or, if you are an accomplished speaker, maybe you share a video or clip on social media or your site.

What's the main difference between people who aren't savvy on social media and those who are? Chances are, you think people are savvy simply because they are online in the first place. That's it. For most people, social media is watching the back-and-forth of a conversation or commenting on an article or news story. They have the guts to put themselves out there online for everyone to see. It is very difficult to distinguish how individual people use social media unless you specifically set out to track them alone. For the most part, people follow the masses. With how busy so many people are nowadays, hardly anyone has the time to examine every post and comment a person makes online. And if someone does notice the content you share, maybe you gain a friend or following because of it. Depending on your subject matter, people may look to you as a thought leader. And if you are perceived as a thought leader in the area you work in, then you, my friend, are becoming a fully-fledged Digital Natural.

CHAPTER 7

THE PILLARS OF INDESTRUCTIBILITY

The secret to surviving and thriving when operating a brand, managing your own brand or reputation, or running business without running afoul of an online mob, is following a set of principles that strengthen the character of a person and, by extension, their brand, reputation, or business.

There are seven pillars of indestructibility: honesty, humility, genuineness, transparency, responsiveness, relevance, and accountability. Leading with these core values will help you navigate the new environment and digital landscape in ways that older, outdated paradigms will not.

The pillars are supported by a foundation of strong values. If the head of an organization leads with these seven pillars but refuses to embrace a value system for managing a customer-centric or employee-empowered business, for example, then the reputation is at risk of collapsing on itself. Indestructibility cannot be attained if the values of an organization are weak.

HONESTY

Serving as the center pillar, honesty sets the foundation for success for anyone who places it as an integral part of their value system in their business or organization. Without it, relationships with stakeholders will always be on shaky ground.

For decades, businesses and organizations relied on the public's acceptance of the idea that no organization needed to tell the public how they were run. Of course, some of these businesses, some leaders, were a little less than honest, but for the most part, no one would know if they were. The press kept the less-than-honest activities from the public. In politics, commerce, entertainment, the military—wherever there was a leader, they were assumed honest unless proven otherwise. With a lack of transparency, the standard operational procedure was to carry on—whether above board or not—and keep the organization moving.

But with the onset of the callout generation, the standard way of doing business has been turned upside down. All organizations and leaders are now expected to throw open the doors to their businesses and let the public in. If the organization is led from an honest place and from an honest leader, then that business will soar in the twenty-first century.

Leading with honesty doesn't have to intrude into the personal space. When people hear the word honesty, they bristle at the initial implication that it means they need to open up the doors to everything about their life and their business. The key to honest leadership, of course, is operating a business with integrity and by the books. But honesty to the modern-age leader means letting the customer know how your honesty impacts how you do business with them.

To lead with honestly means you lead with the customer in mind first—and in the process, your personal ethics and integrity are implied. Any successful business in the modern age must have an honest leader.

HUMILITY

Nothing sets the modern audience's teeth on edge like arrogance in the face of accusation of wrongdoing. However, the effects of humility on your reputation are immeasurable. This is the accountability quotient: without humility, I can almost guarantee the crisis you're trying to manage will go sideways in a hurry. Consider the response of arrogant wrong doers like Harvey Weinstein. The former successful and prolific film producer famously sparked the #MeToo social media campaign after numerous sexual abuse allegations against him came to light. All his attempts to deny, intimidate, and bully his more than eighty female victims resulted in a sentence of twenty-three years in prison. No matter what your response is, if the public perceives it as arrogant, there will be repercussions.

A public already incensed about accused misdeeds is not going to be mollified with an arrogant or dismissive answer. Denying the possibility that you or your organization might have made a mistake will only serve to throw more fuel on the fire. Act without humility, and the public will make you pay the price for your arrogant behavior.

GENUINENESS

In many instances, the concept of authenticity is so closely tied to honesty that many people assume they are the same. Yet that's not necessarily the case, since you can be honest about what you and your organization have been doing yet neglect discussing your actions or behavior in an authentic manner free of pretense.

For the modern-age leader, authenticity means nothing more than being a genuine article—showing people the real you. It's not an easy description to share with leaders, but it's the idea of living your business life like a reality show we watch on television. Leaders, especially the ones who grew up watching black and white television, have been forced to accept this new way of doing business. It certainly isn't easy for many people to accept, but hasn't every generation had to accept one form of abrupt change in how the world is run? But if you've ever watched reality television, you know there is a script. The producer (the leader) must let people into the narrative they want to reveal to the audience. The public doesn't expect to be let into all aspects of your life; they are content with recognizing the parts that relate to them as a customer. But showing a little bit of the private side of your life helps when it complements the professional side.

Authenticity, in a phrase, is showing the good, the bad, and the ugly of running a business. Show customers the raw when it helps you build your story as a leader. Letting the customer in is another form of honesty.

How does this reveal itself in a leader? If you are writing a letter from "the desk of" a leader about an issue facing the business, let the customer in on the why of your position. Ideally, let the reason behind how you manage that issue come from a story from your past, from your personal history. It gives insight to you as a person and shows the customer that you care about what they think of you and the business.

I've used this tactic for some of my clients when they were faced with an issue with their organization or in their role—and some were dealing with big-time issues, like "*The New York Times* and NBC News are calling" types of crises.

Whenever I create a plan for a client dealing with a full-blown crisis (or any type of issues management, for that matter), I tell them to let the public in a little to provide context for their response. Recently, I worked with a client who was the head of an association that involved animals. When an issue made headlines over the treatment of these animals, this leader needed a way to display that they, and their organization, shared a deep love for the care and welfare of these animals. It didn't matter what the issue was, but when PETA accuses your organization of being a threat to animals, the public and the press listen.

Part of the overall strategy to convey that this association cared for the animals' welfare was to share the leader's personal story. In his "Letter from the CEO," we focused on his love of animals, and at the end of the letter, we added a photo of him with his beloved animal and posted the whole thing on the organization's website. It was a simple optic to let the public (and the press, and the activists) know that this was not a cold, heartless leader who did not care for animals. The secondary agenda was to send a message to the latter activists that this organization was not going to take the idea of animal abuse lightly. These signals may be subtle to the average newsreader, but they are critical when waging a battle over your reputation. You have to let your opponent know that you are aware of their battle plan and are up for a fight. Here, the leader's authentic love of animals added another perspective for the public to consider. Authenticity is effective, and I always look for places where I can tell the leader's story.

TRANSPARENCY

If there was ever a buzzword for the whole idea of the modern-age leader, it is this one—transparency. Just as the values of honest and authenticity link, transparency has a strong tie with authenticity as well.

By loose definition, transparency is the ability to see through something, or insufficient cover. It's the idea of letting the light in, and it's typically associated with business policies and procedures. The US Government in the Sunshine Act was a prescription for shedding light on a bill; the same theory applies to organizations that work directly with consumers. Transparency is especially important in regard to consumers—and money. People want to know how the operations of a business affect the consumer's bottom line.

As many leaders are finding out, their current climate does not support a business mindset of covering up. Any form of misdirection or withholding information from the public is not well-received. Almost every front-page story of a business in crisis in 2018 and much of 2019 has an element of cover-up.

- Facebook's privacy policy and leaking users' information to advertisers, and the Russians.
- President Trump's and his team's alleged connection to the Russians in the lead-up to the election.
- Boeing denying that it had informed the pilots of the 737 Max of the software program change, which resulted in the deaths of more than 500 people on two flights.
- Wells Fargo covering for the fake credit cards employees opened from customers' information without approval.

The list goes on. When something is afoot, the press and the public—or a hybrid of the two—will uncover the real story. And more often than not, the problem lies with a leader or a segment of the leadership team who attempted to cover up or keep critical information from the public.

The cover-up—as I have observed time and time again in headline stories and in the industries I work with—does not fly with consumers anymore. Any person who is party to a plan that involves hindering the release of information that can legally and rightfully be shared with the public will be party to its potential downfall.

Of course, there is no way of knowing which organizations get away with hiding information from the public, but as soon as the public gets wind of a cover-up, there's *always* a backlash. Covering, shielding, withholding—it's just another form of lying from the public's perception.

Here's the truth of the matter:

- A lie is always worse than the reveal.
- The painful truth is like a Band-Aid: rip it off and get it over with as soon as possible.

Think of the people in your life who have lied to you or the people you know to be liars. For me, sometimes it seems like they put more energy into covering the lie than it would take to act honestly in the first place. It's a golden rule in parenting, in business and, of course, in the life.

RESPONSIVENESS

There's no time like the present when it comes to responding to issues affecting either your or your organization's reputation. Your responses have to be timely when it comes to announcing press releases or publishing statements. If the negative event in question happens in the public space, you don't have the luxury of taking your time to craft the perfect response; you must post something immediately. If the public knows, and there is no response from you or your organization, then the public will begin to jump to conclusions—and will probably assume you're hoping to hide something. Here, responsiveness and transparency work hand in hand, as the absence of responsiveness is a key indicator of a cover-up.

However, beware of being too quick to respond if you are not prepared to do so. When the signal goes off that your name or business is ping-ponging around the Twitterverse or on Facebook, the reflexive human reaction may be to jump in with a response to quell the chatter. Move too quickly without a proper response at the ready, and you'll trigger a second crisis to contend with at the same time. Crisis management means working through a framework of researching what is being said, planning where and how you need to respond, making the response, and then watching the reaction. If the initial response was inadequate, add a second response if necessary. The key is to be quick—but not without considering every aspect of the response.

Be responsive, not impulsive.

RELEVANCE

Finally, your responses to negative events need to be relevant. They need to reach the right people. If you have a statement, ensure that you post it to social media, and have it shared prominently. Press releases need to be sent to more than news outlets; the public needs to have access to them as well. In times past, it might have been standard operating procedure to allow a news organization to vet and filter news, but today in the digital age, the need isn't as significant. The public dissemination of news through online publications like blogs and social media serve as a network of news services, so put the news out there for everyone to see in places where people can see it.

Relevance goes further than simply releasing statements and drafting press releases accessible across social media. I'll discuss this in more detail later, but leaders should also have a regular social media presence—an active LinkedIn profile at a minimum. It goes without saying that this account, and any other "personal" social media accounts you feel comfortable using, should be maintained with an eye towards transparency, honesty, and authenticity as well. You're the public face of your organization, so you need to act like it. Don't want to manage a personal social media account like Twitter? Make sure your organization itself has one. It still serves as a social mouthpiece when you need it.

ACCOUNTABILITY

The last pillar comes in this order, not because it's the least important, but because it can never be forgotten. Accountability, when overlooked in a crisis, is usually the primary reason why a person or a brand cannot recover from a cancellation.

Full stop.

The lack of accountability, even in someone's personal life, is the key indicator that the negotiations will not favor the accused.

Understand that a person's initial reaction to any accusation—true or not—is a reflexive pushback either in the form of a denial or blame. Resisting an attack is a natural human behavior. However, with the rapid speed of social media and the constant temperature checks on a reputation when a person or a brand runs afoul, the public and the press have little patience for passing blame, excuses, or denials.

I've noticed in the months after the COVID-19 pandemic, the public's patience for selfish or bad behavior that spills out online has decreased significantly. During the #MeToo movement, it seemed as if the reputational spiral would spin downwards over a course of weeks, if not months. As the strain of quarantines and social distancing mixed with politics in the lead up to the 2020 presidential election, it came as no surprise when the story of George Floyd's deadly arrest from an officer with the Minneapolis Police Department erupted into riots and protests.

The midpoint of 2020 was a collision of pain and anger that naturally found its way onto social media.

You could feel it and see it online: no matter the event—people were now demanding accountability from the following:

- The press.
- The President of the United States.
- The Minneapolis Police.
- The Government.
- Anyone or any entity that allowed a virus to spread into a pandemic.
- The 'Karens' who were filmed screaming at grocery store workers who demanded they wear a mask to shop. The impatience for an organization's or a specific person's lack of accountability is the accelerant that usually fuels a PR crisis.

Since the start of the COVID-19 pandemic, there were numerous instances of social media users piling on a well-known name from an uncovered misdeed from the past or an unfortunate micro-moment that seemed to escalate into a full-fledged drama in a matter of a few trending minutes.

Several celebrities, brands, and companies were denounced in the irritable months after the initial outbreaks in March 2020.

To examine the impact of accountability, let's take a look at three "cancel" incidents affecting talk show hosts.

Ellen DeGeneres

The comedian sparked extreme backlash (#CancelEllen) when she compared isolating in her multi-million-dollar mansion to being in prison during a monologue while filming at home for her talk show in April 2020. DeGeneres faced a second wave of a bad press when a Twitter thread started from this tweet by comedian Kevin T. Porter (@KevinTPorter):

Kevin T. Porter ✅
@KevinTPorter

Right now we all need a little kindness. You know, like Ellen Degeneres always talks about! 😊 💚

She's also notoriously one of the meanest people alive

Respond to this with the most insane stories you've heard about Ellen being mean & I'll match every one w/ $2 to @LAFoodBank

1:12 PM · Mar 20, 2020 · Twitter for iPhone

Messages poured into the thread with various negative stories about the talk show. Not surprising, the thread caught the eye of the press and Ellen had a massive PR crisis on her hands. Since then, *The Ellen DeGeneres Show* has fallen under heavy scrutiny for how the host has treated employees in the past.

Reports came flying in about the working conditions that many employees have been experiencing while filming the show. Many of which include racism and intimidation. Ellen's reputation was sinking as the tweets and commentary kept building.

After six months of silence, Ellen finally released an official statement on the reports.

Below is DeGeneres's full letter to her staff:

Hey everybody—it's Ellen. On day one of our show, I told everyone in our first meeting that *The Ellen DeGeneres Show* would be a place of happiness—no one would ever raise their voice, and everyone would be treated with respect. Obviously, something changed, and I am disappointed to learn that this has not been the case. And for that, I am sorry. Anyone who knows me knows it's the opposite of what I believe and what I hoped for our show.

I could not have the success I've had without all of your contributions. My name is on the show and everything we do and I take responsibility for that. Alongside Warner Bros, we immediately began an internal investigation and we are taking steps, together, to correct the issues. As we've grown exponentially, I've not been able to stay on top of everything and relied on others to do their jobs as they knew I'd want them done. Clearly some didn't. That will now change and I'm committed to ensuring this does not happen again.

I'm also learning that people who work with me and for me are speaking on my behalf and misrepresenting who I am and that has to stop. As someone who was judged and nearly lost everything for just being who I am, I truly understand and have deep compassion for those being looked at differently, or treated unfairly, not equal, or—worse—disregarded. To think that any one of you felt that way is awful to me.

It's been way too long, but we're finally having conversations about fairness and justice. We all have to be more mindful about the way our words and actions affect others, and I'm glad the issues at our show were brought to my attention. I promise to do my part in continuing to push myself and everyone around me to learn and grow. It's important to me and to Warner Bros. that everyone who has something to say can speak up and feels safe doing so.

I am so proud of the work we do and the fun and joy we all help put out in the world. I want everyone at home to love our show and I want everyone who makes it to love working on it. Again, I'm so sorry to anyone who didn't have that experience. If not for COVID, I'd have done this in person, and I can't wait to be back on our stage and see you all then.

Stay safe and healthy.

Love,

Ellen

The subtext of the letter was clear. Ellen was not going to shoulder any of the blame of this PR debacle. Instead, she sidestepped the blame and placed it firmly on the backs of her producers. So much for the show being a place for people to tune in for a daily dose of kindness.

However, even the best written statement can't stop the groundswell of negative publicity if the person at the center of the crisis refuses to acknowledge their role. For months Ellen continued to remain silent, which allowed the negative publicity to fester even further.

Ellen needed a plan.

The plan she chose (or some team chose for her) was silence.

For the record, unless there are compelling reasons—like legal—for not responding to charges made public, silence is never a good plan. Especially when your fans and critics alike can speak on your behalf. A vacuum created by silence is often filled with other's opinion—and it's rarely forgiving.

Ellen finally decided to break the silence and address the allegations in her opening monologue at the start of her eighteenth season.

Now why did Ellen choose to finally speak up on her program? My crisis-management brain says she wanted a safe environment on her home turf, the studio. Ellen wanted a forum where she could apologize in a scripted format, not a sit-down interview with a reporter. No way. She needed to remain in control in order to make this right. It was a format where she could deploy her most strategic weapon, her humor.

However, the monologue was stiff, and Ellen looked uncomfortable throughout the delivery. Worse, because of the pandemic, Ellen had to perform it in front of a studio audience of monitors with guests watching virtually. Not an ideal environment for rehabilitating the image of a comedian and talk show host.

Jimmy Fallon

This second talk show host found himself in a Twitter funk when the #JimmyFallonIsOver started trending in June 2020. A "black face" controversy erupted from a resurfaced *Saturday Night Live* sketch from two decades ago when Fallon impersonated Chris Rock in "black face" makeup. Fallon immediately apologized on Twitter and also spoke to several experts on his program about racial inequality, including the president and CEO of the NAACP, Derrick Johnson.

Jimmy Kimmel

Another Jimmy in the social backlash soup (#CancelKimmel) was late night host Jimmy Kimmel. It was revealed the host of *Jimmy Kimmel Live* had used "black face" to impersonate celebrities like Karl Malone and Oprah Winfrey on a previous show he co-hosted with Adam Carolla called *The Man Show,* a Comedy Central series he starred in from 1999 to 2003. Just before the crisis started to pick up steam online, Kimmel announced he was taking a summer hiatus. "My family is healthy, I'm healthy. I just need a couple of months off," the statement read. Only a few years ago, the public might have bought the excuse. But in the age of the cancel culture, the tone and timing of the statement meant something was afoot.

After weeks of criticism, Kimmel finally issued an apology: "That delay was a mistake. There is nothing more important to me than your respect, and I apologize to those who were genuinely hurt or offended by the makeup I wore or the words I spoke."

Three reputation casualties of the cancel culture. Each celebrity took a massive hit to their reputation, but to what extent is difficult to determine without ratings and advertising dollars lost. However, all three hosts—targeted during a span of a few short months—were in similar crises but responded with vastly different manners.

1. Ellen DeGeneres: No response. *Denial*
2. Jimmy Fallon: Immediate apology on social media and then a follow-up *mea culpa* and race-centric interviews on his television program. *Rebuild*
3. Jimmy Kimmel: Delayed apology. Used the phrasing, "I apologize to those who were genuinely hurt or offended by the makeup I wore or the words I spoke." *Diminish*

Crisis-response strategies are not fool-proof, but the results often follow a pattern. The clearest path to indestructibly is one that takes on the most accountability.

The denial tactic seeks to remove or disconnect the person from the crisis. The diminish strategy accepts only partial responsibility. The rebuilding strategy starts from a position of accountability to reform a foundation of trust.

All three hosts may still be on the air (for now), but only one host chose to respond with full accountability. A person should never gamble their reputation by squirming out of a crisis without fully owning up to it. If I were in Vegas, my money would be on Jimmy Fallon to survive this crisis in the long run and remain on the air. My prediction for *The Ellen DeGeneres Show* is a wrap before its twentieth season. The ratings for the program are in a freefall and the public has yet to reembrace Ellen 2.0.

WHY PEOPLE ARE CANCELLED

"Cancel Culture" has become so pervasive that the term is now firmly established in online lexicon. The idea of canceling a person or a brand is often derided online by people who note the randomness and unfairness of the online mob of overly judgmental people who don't seem to have better things to do with their time.

If you are one of those people, think again.

The online shunning is not random nor is it unfair. The people who are targeted for cancellation or the brands that find themselves in the public's crosshairs are in that position for a reason. The outrage is typically not from the questionable act that took the notice of the public, but from an inadequate response to the questionable act. The blowback is caused by a collective repudiation of the response itself or the hubris behind it.

Outrage can spread so quickly online that the thought of jumping in with a response can be terrifying for anyone or any brand trying to stop the momentum, that staying silent can feel like a safe harbor. Don't be tempted to wait it out because a PR crisis waits for no man.

A response acknowledging the role of the targeted person, business, or brand is the only course for navigating the crisis. A crisis festers and spreads in an environment of silence. Respond quickly and respond with accountability. Without it, people will pounce, and the outrage will be amplified.

Accepting accountability without a hint of ego, arrogance, or narcissism increases the chances of survival. Diminish, dismiss, shift the blame, or use any high-handedness, and—all of a sudden—you're cancelled.

Acknowledge fully what you did, what you said, what you wrote, or what was captured on film. Don't hide behind excuses or obfuscate within an inch of your life. Social media has a way of uncovering liars— quickly. If you show remorse and take accountability for your actions, the public is more likely to give you a break and move onto the next cancellation. However, showing partial accountability by only apologizing to the people you offended, or offering no statement at all—well, good luck to you.

CRACKS IN THE FOUNDATION

A solid foundation for an organization is formed when there is an awareness of its culture from outside and from within. The system of values and doctrine should be shaped before a crisis to create the solid foundational footing to survive it. If the culture is toxic, chances are the backlash of a crisis will be as well.

When the COVID-19 pandemic was in full swing, the companies that displayed their commitment to their employees' mental well-being and economic livelihood received the benefit of customer goodwill, and, as we saw every day in the first few weeks of quarantine, positive press. Both people and the press alike were quick to share inspirational stories from leaders who sacrificed for the sake of their employees. The global pandemic was a Black Swan event that few organizations, if any, were prepared for. But the organizations with strong values and a positive culture were able to survive and sustain themselves through such a challenging and unpredictable time.

Corporate and organization culture was exposed again months later when displaying support for the Black Lives Matter movement through statements. Statements and leaders speaking out about the need for racial equality were the next litmus test for culture and values.

- Was a statement shared on social media?
- Did the CEO make a statement and share it to both external and internal stakeholders?
- How frequently did the organization make statements? Was it a one and done or an ongoing conversation?

If the first half of 2020 showed us anything, it's that a company's culture and value system is open for everyone to see during a time of crisis—like the pandemic or issues of race—or when a company is in crisis. One of the most valuable tactics for managing a crisis is letting people know how you treat the people from within and the values your leadership and organization holds. A caring culture is key to building indestructibility.

CREATING AND MAINTAINING A RELATIONSHIP WITH YOUR CUSTOMERS

One factor that is critical to the reputation of your company is how your leaders and employees are viewed in the public's eye. Here are some key fundamentals to keep in mind.

1. The public needs to trust you.
2. The public needs to feel like they are getting something in return.
3. You need to have a value system that aligns with the customer.

4. Your mission statement needs to show your dedication to your customers. Take, for example, the mission statement for Southwest Airlines: "The mission of Southwest Airlines is dedication to the highest quality of customer service delivered with a sense of warmth, friendliness, individual pride, and company spirit."[7]
5. Your company culture should reflect your customer-centric mission statement.
6. Your company culture should reflect an employee-centric value system.

---

7. "About Southwest," Southwest Airlines. https://www.southwest.com/html/about -southwest/index.html.

CHAPTER 8

THE INDESTRUCTIBLE FORMULA FOR DEALING WITH A CRISIS

The rules for crisis response have changed drastically over the past two decades. When I started my career at FEMA, the national press was at the top of the list of stakeholders who held the greatest sway over reputation and public opinion. However, in today's crisis communications ecosystem, the influence of social media often determines the outcome.

Not only has real-time social media sped up the clock on crisis response, the results are delivered in real-time as well. Oftentimes, the people who are in crisis or represent a brand in crisis are learning about it at the same time as their stakeholders. Social media has also created new categories for crisis:

- Angry customers
- Leadership faux pas
- Organizational social media fails
- Self-inflicted crises
- Resurfaced offensive social media posts
- Bad behavior

Social media has played an increasingly critical role in the outcome of a crisis for people and brands. For one reason, that's where everyone goes when there is a crisis. As a Gen Xer, a newspaper app is usually the first place I go when I catch wind of a crisis unfolding, but I quickly move to Twitter to get a broader view of the situation.

With tweets and trending hashtags comingling with published news articles, the dynamics of a critical situation change quickly when opinion is introduced into the mix. It doesn't take long before a full-scale crisis is playing out in real-time for the online world to follow.

In my experience working with clients either mitigating or responding to a crisis, as much as I wish it were the case (for planning purposes), no two crises are the same. A crisis can fall into a category, but any crisis can create its own narrative from the hashtag to the type of information shared online. A "resurfaced quote" crisis requires a different response than a "CEO caught on video doing something illegal" crisis. However, the winning formula for managing a crisis in a social media environment seems to follow a pattern—one that I have identified as the new rules for reputation management used by famous brands and people as well as my own clients.

HOW TO BUILD AN INDESTRUCTIBLE RESPONSE

There are only three main steps in the response framework.[8]

Step One: Own it. You must acknowledge, accept, or apologize. This step simply requires you to tell the truth. It's also the step many people skip, which leads to a bigger or longer-lasting crisis. The public and the press will notice the absence of Step One and will point it out.

Step Two: Clarify it. Put the issue into context. After acknowledging the truth, you can lessen some of the damage by providing background or context. You're creating breathing room to explain things in depth and framing your response.

Step Three: Promise it. Announce your commitment to plans, priorities, and changes to come. Finally, explain how and when you will change for the better. This is the redemption step: "I will do my best to do this or that."

---

8. I am a big believer in the power of three. To quote one of the songs from my childhood soundtrack on Saturday morning, "Three is the magic number." Members of Generation X know what I'm writing about here.

If you follow all three steps, in order, you can move to a bonus step: **You win it.**

Here's an example: In February 2019, Virginia Governor Ralph Northam (D) made news when photographs from his Eastern Virginia Medical School yearbook were published on a right-wing website. The photos from Northam's page showed a black-and-white image of two unidentified people, one in blackface and the other wearing a Ku Klux Klan hood.

As far as crises go, this is on the extreme end. Race is a third rail of American policies. It is difficult to preserve a favorable reputation when you have been called a racist or when evidence on social media suggests you're a racist. And photographic evidence is among the hardest to explain or contradict.

Northam responded with a statement the same day:

> "Earlier today, a website published a photograph of me from my 1984 medical school yearbook in a costume that was clearly racist and offensive. I am deeply sorry for the decision I made to appear as I did in this photo and for the hurt that decision caused then and now. This behavior is not in keeping with who I am today and the values I have fought for throughout my career in the military, in medicine, and in public service. But I want to be clear, I understand how this decision shakes Virginians' faith in that commitment. I recognize that it will take time and serious effort to heal the damage this conduct has caused. I am ready to do that important work. The first step is to offer my sincerest apology and to state my absolute commitment to living up to the expectations Virginians set for me when they elected me to be their Governor."[9]

Northam's response touches on all three steps:

Step One: Own it. "I am deeply sorry for the decision I made to appear as I did in this photo and for the hurt that decision caused then and now. . . . The first step is to offer my sincerest apology and to state my absolute commitment to living up to the expectations Virginians set for me when they elected me to be their Governor."

---

9. "Va. Gov. Northam's yearbook pic of men in blackface, Klan robe spurs calls for his resignation." *NBC News.* February 1, 2019.

Step Two: Clarify it. "This behavior is not in keeping with who I am today and the values I have fought for throughout my career in the military, in medicine, and in public service."

Step Three: Promise it. "I recognize that it will take time and serious effort to heal the damage this conduct has caused. I am ready to do that important work."

Depending on the situation, and if you've followed all the other steps, that fourth step may be appropriate.

Step Four: Win it. Here is where Gov. Northam asked for something in return since he adhered to the first three steps. I know what you're thinking: It takes a lot of nerve to ask the public for something in return when you created the crisis to begin with. But if done well, it works *and* it alters the conversation in favor of the person doing the asking.

In Gov. Northam's case, here is the ask, subtle though it may be:

> "I am ready to do that important work. The first step is to offer my sincerest apology and to state my absolute commitment to living up to the expectations Virginians set for me when they elected me to be their Governor."

The ask was to let him remain as the governor of Virginia. Of course, it's not as if this were an episode of *America's Got Talent* with four Virginians on a panel deciding whether to send Northam on to the next round or home. Northam is asking for the public and the press not to call for his resignation—and also letting everyone know that he doesn't plan to leave. It's a test balloon to see how to approach the next phase of the scandal, but also a bit of a power play—forcing those who would remove him to up the ante if they really want him gone.

As of this writing, Gov. Northam is still in office.

DON'T UNDERESTIMATE THE APOLOGY

The pushback I hear most often about Step One is the liability. Saying "I'm sorry" is the most complex piece of the Indestructible Framework because it is the one area people or brands in trouble want to avoid for legal reasons. Accepting responsibility can result in the losing end of a lawsuit.

Yes, a person or a brand must be careful when using the term *apologize*; however, it does not mean it should be avoided at all cost.

Frame the word by replacing the word *fault* with *responsibility*. Expressing remorse is a way to acknowledge your role while attached to the issue. An apology is critical to rebuilding a reputation because it recognizes some rule was violated and shows respect to people impacted or victimized by an incident. The downside to the *mea culpa* is that it does attach blame to someone or some entity, but it blunts the impact of a greater crisis without it.

Incompetence and mistakes need an apology. The public needs to understand that a leader recognizes the mistake and will make necessary changes. Accepting accountability may seem risky, but it's far riskier from a reputational point of view to try and avoid it.

How *Not* to Apologize

It's important not to view the apology as the failsafe to any crisis that guarantees redemption. Partial, insincere, or non-apology apologies increase the anger and negative chatter online, which intensifies the damaging press.

For example, in the fall of 2019 Shane Gillis was tapped as one of three new featured players on *Saturday Night Live*. That is, until a resurfaced video from 2018 showed him using a racial slur during a podcast interview. It went like this: "Chinatown's (expletive) nuts," Gillis said. "Let the (expletive) live there," he added, using a racial slur.

"I'm a comedian who pushes boundaries. I sometimes miss," he wrote in a statement posted to Twitter. "I'm happy to apologize to anyone who's actually offended by anything I've said."[10]

His apology continued: "If you go through my 10 years of comedy, most of it bad, you're going to find a lot of bad misses. . . . My intention is never to hurt anyone, but I am trying to be the best comedian I can be and sometimes that requires risks."

No one wants an apology to come back to haunt them. For Shane Gillis it did in the form of getting dumped from the cast of *Saturday Night Live* before the season premiere.

Gillis's partial apology of "I'm happy to apologize to anyone who's actually offended by anything I've said," was not only partial but snarky. Chances are Gillis would have been sliced from the SNL cast regardless of the sincerity of the apology, but the chances of him getting hired again in some other venue would be greater if he had written an apology showing actual remorse instead of a flippant partial attempt.

To Gillis's credit, he tried again.[11]

The second attempt went over about as well as the first one.

10. Gillis, Shane. Twitter Post. September 12, 2019, 10:43 PM.
11. Gillis, Shane. Twitter Post. September 16, 2019, 2:11 PM. https://twitter.com/Shanemgillis/status/1173690932832505856.

For anyone who thinks a partial apology is the lesser of two evils over a full one, Google Shane Willis on IMDb.com to learn the last time he was recorded working in entertainment.

Senator Al Franken

Here's an example of how you can still blow an apology even after you hire a crisis team to draft a message. Franken sat down for an exclusive interview with Esme Murphy, a reporter from WCCO, the CBS television affiliate in his home state of Minnesota. During the interview, Franken said:

> "I am a warm person and I hug people, and in some of these encounters, these pictures or meetings, some women—and any is too many—have felt that I have crossed a line. And I am terribly sorry about that."[12]

This part of the interview worked. Apologies are the critical and essential first step when trying to win back the public's trust following a misdeed. Sen. Franken did so and added the strong talking point "and any is too many."

But then the hedging started.

> "As I said, I take thousands of photos. I don't remember these particular photos. But I think that women experience . . . my intent doesn't matter. My recollection of that kiss is different from hers."

This didn't work. An audience can accept that someone in Franken's position wouldn't remember each of the thousands of photos taken during his time in public life. But, as Murphy noted in her questioning, all those watching the interview would expect him to remember each and every time he inappropriately touched a woman's behind. Every. Time.

Franken's Democratic colleagues in the Senate called for his resignation, and he obliged.

---

12. "'I Am Just Very Sorry': Franken to Return to Work Monday." *CBS Minnesota.* November 26, 2017.

Louis CK

Louis CK's career was on a roll until he was swept up in the #MeToo Movement in 2017. The comedian was accused of inappropriate sexual behavior from several women. Being the edgy comedian, Louis CK tried an edgy apology to ward off the bad press. Perhaps it was an attempt to garner support from his fans—or anyone he thought had an edgy sense of humor like him.

He started out fine—excellent in fact—because he said in his statement, "These stories are true."

But then he let the edge in:

"At the time, I said to myself that what I did was O.K. because I never showed a woman my dick without asking first, which is also true. But what I learned later in life, too late, is that when you have power over another person, asking them to look at your dick isn't a question. It's a predicament for them. The power I had over these women is that they admired me. And I wielded that power irresponsibly. I have been remorseful of my actions. And I've tried to learn from them. And run from them. Now I'm aware of the extent of the impact of my actions."[13]

Uh, yeah . . . using the foul language to remain "on brand" in an apology confirmed two things: Louis CK is bad at apologies and is likely *a dick* in real life. Louis CK is attempting a comeback, doing standup in small auditoriums in remote towns. And he's having trouble selling tickets.

The last word on The Apology: if you are in a position of deciding if an apology is necessary during a crisis, chances are, it is.

---

13. "Louis C.K. Admits to Sexual Misconduct as Media Companies Cut Ties." *The New York Times*. November 10, 2017. https://www.nytimes.com/2017/11/10/movies/louis-ck-i-love-you-daddy-release-is-canceled.html.

HOW TO RESPOND WHEN YOU ARE UNDER ATTACK OR ANTICIPATE AN ATTACK

1. **Know where you stand.**
   Do not start the apology or acknowledgment without first testing the waters. Google your name. Look at what people are saying about you or the issue on social media. If the sharks are in the water, don't throw them bloody meat. Understanding the public's and your stakeholders' sentiment is critical at this stage.

2. **Atone as humbly as possible.**
   This is another place where the ego gets in the way of the apology. Don't hedge, don't quibble with details. Be sincere in your message. If you don't want to say or write the words "I'm sorry," then be as empathetic to those accusing you as humanly possible.

3. **Quick, quick, lickity split.**
   If the public is anxiously awaiting this apology, then get it out as soon as you can. Get your facts first—all of them—and address as many as you can in summary in Step One.

4. **Speak to the hoi polloi.**
   Speak to your stakeholders in a language they understand. Speak clearly and as jargon-free as possible. Watch your words. If a passenger on your airline was too aggressively manhandled off the plane, they were not "re-accommodated"; they were forcibly removed.

5. **Respond where people are: online.**
   Written statements alone are for people or organizations who are not apologizing. They are reporting an event that requires no follow-up. Think of a public divorce. But a screw up that affects stakeholders needs to be addressed where the stakeholders consume information. A video on a widely shared platform is the best way to respond in this case. Keep it brief, make it subtitled, and make it sincere.

NO ONE IS TOO IMPORTANT TO USE SOCIAL MEDIA

In this modern era, when your personal or professional work could be exposed online to the public at any time, leaders must abide by a certain set of rules. To do otherwise risks finding themselves on the other side of their customers' wrath—or worse, exposed to the tender ministrations of the public.

This requires maintaining a social media presence online. It's hard work, and I often hear the excuses why people don't want to be online: *I have better things to do with my time! I can't keep up with everything online, why should I even try?* There's also my personal favorite: *I'm too busy/important for social media!* This last one is epic because it heavily implies that social media is beneath them—which is ironic, since social media can become the vehicle of downfall for organizations or individuals who underestimate its power.

News flash: your own ignorance and inability to adapt will be your downfall. If you want to survive the new normal of creating and maintaining a professional reputation, you need to learn the ins and outs of the playbook for digital leadership. Here are the tactics you need to master:

Get to Know Your (Potentially) Biggest Advocates: Your Employees

Ivory tower leadership can be damaging to an organization. Don't assume because you own a business that everyone likes you or even respects you. Paychecks are *expected* by employees, not earned. Respect and admiration are something *leaders* need to earn. Take the time to get to know everyone you manage.

When I worked with an owner and operator of a successful enterprise of hotels and fitness clubs, I asked him if he ever thought of auditioning for *Undercover Boss,* the television series where the head of a business dons a disguise to works among the employees in an effort to learn about their business on the ground floor. The profile of his business seemed like the right size and with the spread of locations, he seemed like the perfect guy to pull it off. He told me numerous people over the years asked him about appearing on the show and his answer is always the same: *"If my employees can't recognize me with a wig and glasses on, then I have no business running my business. I need them to know me."*

Tone Down the Ego

This one is arguably the most important facet of surviving a social media apocalypse. It's also one of the most difficult skills to master when it comes to business owners, C-level executives, or anyone else in positions of power. Letting your ego run wild and entertaining thoughts of being above reproach due to your lofty position is almost certainly going to be your undoing. The internet is the great equalizer, and social media has brought more than a few people to their knees, despite their seemingly untouchable egos.

Suspend Judgment of Others

It's all too easy to immediately go on the offensive when you feel like you or your organization has been attacked. Yet lashing out and attacking your accusers—whether they're personal or professional—will paint a negative picture for the public. Throwing around judgmental, angry, and accusatory language at whistleblowers or other individuals only shows you're more interested in destroying your attackers than anything else. That vengeful attitude makes onlookers believe you're acting out of guilt and that you have something to hide.

Acknowledge Your Role and Validate the Public's Response

Remember, authenticity, honesty, and transparency are all integral parts of responding to a crisis of reputation. You can acknowledge the fact that you or your organization has become embroiled in an issue, and you should do so in ways that validate the anger, fear, or other emotional responses of the public. You can accomplish all this without appearing dismissive of any accusations made or evidence presented. Treat the issue as seriously as you can, as this sends a clear message to the public: we hear your concerns, and we're going to address them.

Don't Hedge

Once you've drafted an initial statement to mention you will address the crisis, it's time to write an official and binding response. In times like these, if you or your organization has been caught red-handed (or are even being called out for behavior that can be interpreted as unethical or immoral), it's time for a public apology. Don't hedge in your statements by saying how surprised you were that people were offended, as this makes you look out of touch with reality. Likewise, this is not the time for qualified or parsed statements; half-hearted "for those who were offended, we offer our apologies" are obviously not genuine. Issue a sincere apology to everyone.

Take Responsibility with Real, Actionable Steps

Finally, simply apologizing for actions or behavior that's been called out in public as inappropriate isn't enough. Even a child knows that simply saying you're sorry is worthless unless you change your future behavior. Take responsibility for the crisis by announcing the genuine, actionable steps you or your organization will take to make amends. It goes without saying that this is not the time for token efforts—you'll need to show how serious you are about mending the situation if you expect your reputation to emerge intact without being cancelled.

10 TIPS FOR KEEPING YOUR BRAND— AND YOUR REPUTATION—INTACT

1. **Don't dismiss communicators.** Communicators are not people staring at their phones all day posting to social media, or the people you dump all social media projects on because you don't believe social is an integral part of your business. Both are important! Give your communicators a seat at the table and listen to their contributions. Embrace what they tell you to do regarding your response to criticism. You hired them for a reason. If you don't agree with their premise say: "Tell me more," "What's behind your thinking?", or "Please help me understand."

2. **Fill the vacuum.** Social media waits for no one. Gone are the days of having a full workday to hash out a media statement with a team to drop just before a print deadline. Again, as stated earlier, when a shoe drops, the other one will quickly follow if you don't fill the void with a response. In the absence of a response, someone will make it for you—and it won't be pretty.

3. **Don't overlook your key stakeholders: your employees.** When a story breaks on social media about an organization, typically the first people to get contacted are the employees. They can be your best PR in times of strife. Communicate with these advocates early and often.

4. **Toss aside the previous crisis toolkit.** The toolkit you sprang for in the 2016 budget is outdated. Creating a decision tree and updating it frequently is vital to have in a time of crisis. Having a crisis response app is even better. Also, make sure you create a safe and effective communication channel for the team and employees—like Slack, the collaboration platform. It can be an effective tool for communicating with each other to ensure real-time responses.

5. **Create your quotable quote.** Craft three quotes perfect for the press and succinct enough for social media. Keep the 280-character limit for Twitter.

6. **Tap into authenticity.** Do your customers like you? Hopefully, you've worked on your brand's reputation before the crisis hit. It's a continual effort that you'll need to rely on when it matters.

7. **Do digital.** Use video, audio, and graphics to tell your story. Use your website and social media accounts—all of them—to share it.

8. **Take a polarizing pulse check.** What is happening in the world culturally, morally, and politically? What is going viral and why? Don't be tone-deaf in your messaging and inadvertently cause a negative reaction to your initial response.

9. **Monitor the mentions.** Watch what is happening to your brand and its reputation in real-time. Comment where you can and adjust messaging when necessary.

10. **Don't defend, parse an apology, or pick apart the blowback.** The public wants to see an acknowledgment of your role in the

crisis and accountability. They will move on from the initial crisis if you have a path for redemption.

FAIL TO PLAN, PLAN TO FAIL: CRISIS MANAGEMENT PLANS

If the coronavirus outbreak has taught us anything, it's that no organization or business is immune from a crisis. Everyone working for a business during COVID-19 is in the business of crisis communications.

Crisis communication plans are created by skilled public relations and communication professionals, but everyone should understand that the primary objective of the plan is operational continuity.

Everyone has a hand in keeping the lights on and the doors open. To stay in business, a plan must be in place to communicate to your key stakeholders that you are open for business.

Leaders can cultivate an indestructible culture by ensuring a crisis communication plan is in place.

What belongs in a plan?

A solid crisis communication plan has elements that can be easily implemented by leaders and employees alike but also identifies the organization's vulnerabilities to plan around or fix when a crisis hits.

Accounting for insufficient social media channels, time pressures, limited staff, and budgets can be examples of vulnerabilities.

If I have to pinpoint an area of focus missing from most crisis communication plans residing on a shelf for the past few years, I'd look to online and website components.

So much of a crisis is managed and communicated online. Adequate resources should be in place to prepare online messaging dissemination, implementation, and feedback collection.

Is every plan the same?

A crisis can be universal across all industries, like COVID-19, or geographical in nature, like a hurricane. Any event or issue that ceases or interrupts operations or puts a reputation at risk can be defined as a crisis.

The response plans can be universal in scope, but the response needs customization for the organization's key stakeholders.

How is your organization going to respond to a crisis?

Traditional or new media—or a mix of both? Will leadership write a statement or deliver a response on Facebook Live?

Googling "crisis communication plan" can only get an organization so far. The best crisis communication plans factor in the specific needs of each of the stakeholder groups.

In my opinion, every crisis communication plan for the digital age needs to include a section for leadership communications. Social media has caused the scrutiny level for leaders to increase significantly, which opens the door to reputations being tarnished from the ill-timed or tone-deaf responses.

Crisis communication plans must include a statement for internal stakeholders about the approach to the crisis from the organization's view. Consider it an "all hands on deck" statement stating an objective of communicating accurately and effectively during a crisis.

External stakeholders should receive a statement including value statements and changes to operations via email, social media, and web pages. Written statements by leadership is a mandatory starting point, but recorded or live stream video will get you further down the road of a solid response.

Create templates for press releases, social media, and official statements and update the template as necessary. Identify the official spokespeople for your organization and the key media contacts.

Relevant online channels like social media and web pages need policies in place and structured tasks for employees.

Lastly, don't forget the evaluation phase. It's often overlooked, but it's a critical piece for charting your plans. Solicit feedback from both internal and external stakeholders. Both groups offer valuable advice on the pieces of the plan that work and the ones that fall short.

An unmet threat can be a disenfranchised customer who is waiting to strike out at your business online. A key stakeholder, in many cases, can be the exact stakeholder. That's the one disenfranchised customer who will target a shoddy response by telling everyone online.

How often do I need to update the plan?

The crisis plan is not a static step-by-step guide or a plan that needs updating when people get around to it. The most effective crisis communication plans are treated as living documents that reside online and not in a binder on a shelf collecting dust.

Keep the plan a dynamic one by housing it online in a shared folder for multiple people to access.

Here is the bottom line for leaders: If you have plans in place, they'll help keep you ahead of the fray—and chances are, you will be in the fray at some point.

However you may feel about it personally, today's so-called cancel culture is real. It's here, it's powerful, it can be leveraged to great effect, and if your company is on the receiving end of it, you could potentially be in some deep trouble. As an executive, you need every weapon in your arsenal to ensure you don't fall victim to cancel culture, so here's what you need to know about managing this emergent trend that shows no signs of going away any time soon.

HOW TO AVOID GETTING YOUR OWN COMPANY CANCELLED

It's very hard to stop a runaway train when it doesn't have any brakes. If your company has engaged in something that is perceived as being unjust in some way, or something that people feel needs to be held accountable for, you could be in for a very wild ride. It doesn't matter what other good work you might have done in the past, what types of products or services you provide or their quality—if you're in the crosshairs of an angry generation of disenfranchised youth because of perceived injustice, you're in for a wild ride.

At this point, it doesn't matter if you're guilty of doing something untoward or not. The only way to avoid being buried under a complete avalanche of protests and calls to boycott your company is to face the problem head-on, fully and publicly, and with as much honesty and transparency as possible. Failing to do otherwise in any way will result in that runaway train doing massive damage to your company's reputation. Again, this is regardless of whether the criticisms of your company are valid and justified.

SWALLOWING YOUR PRIDE AND FIXING THE PROBLEM

This probably doesn't seem fair to you. It may not be. Yet whether your company is being given a fair shake is largely irrelevant—this is the new normal when it comes to how a business needs to manage its brand and reputation. You're going to need to swallow your pride. Meeting outrage with outrage is not going to work; no matter how powerful your company might be, you're nothing in the face of an angry mob of consumers who aren't content with simply taking their business elsewhere. If you're combative or dismissive, you'll be cancelled so hard you'll be applying for a job at the local 7-Eleven before you know it.

Your core objective here is to fix the problem, whatever it may be. This means you address the issue head-on, apologize if necessary (and even if it's not necessary), and set out clear, concise goals as to how you'll be fixing the problem. Most of all, you will need to proclaim loudly that your company's culture does not support whatever the issue at hand is, and that you are committed to fixing the problem no matter what it takes.

REBUILDING AND GETTING ON WITH YOUR BUSINESS

This approach to an incipient issue works. Not only that, it can lead to massive rewards for a company that hears its critics and responds accordingly. An excellent example of how this has played out in the past is how ABC fired Roseanne Barr after massive outrage at her posting of a racist comment on her Twitter account. While there were some who decried the move on ABC's part, the results spoke for themselves: ratings for the second season of Roseanne's show, now renamed "The Conners," showed that people were content to tune in to watch a spin off without the person who created the brand in the cast. Over two years later and the program is still on the air.

Any company can end up being targeted by cancel culture. Yet whether you rise above with grace and humility or whether it takes you down with it is entirely up to you and how you respond. As generational cultures continue to shift and change, the writing is on the wall: modern consumers, who are rising to prominence as older generations decline, are known to value honesty and integrity, and they're as willing to reward those who meet their social justice thresholds as much as they are willing to punish any transgressors. Where your company falls on that line is entirely up to you.

The key to indestructibility in the cancel culture is to create an almost impenetrable shield, preventing the negative stories from taking hold.

TRUE NORTH

It seems as if everyone has a value system in place they naturally navigate back to in life and in work. This is the internal compass that guides them successfully through life. It's a setting point that indicates a person's personal mission or a business's reason for being—the unseen power that moves the needle to the same place time and time again.

The "True North" of a business or brand could be tied to a company's values. For example:

- Truth & Transparency

- Customer Service
- Hard Work
- Protecting the Environment

The True North of a leader represents who they are as a human and operates at their deepest and truest level. It is the point that reveals one's values, passions, beliefs, and motivations. Some examples include:

- The CEO of a children's hospital who advocates for more research funding for children.
- A superintendent of a school system who vocally supports LGBTQ students.
- The owner of a chain of gyms who volunteers at local schools to talk about healthy eating for kids.

There is also a True North that reveals itself during a crisis. It is how a company or business leader will react when tested by a public "callout." When a crisis is on the horizon, the needle will settle on the spot representing the way it was always done and accepted in the past.

There is usually a person who is used to being in control and has a habitual or reflexive response to an action, usually when someone or some movement is incongruent to their mission or bottom line.

I work within these margins. I can spot this trouble on the horizon and predict the behaviors and next steps.

Leaders are hard-wired to respond in a certain way, especially based on their backgrounds and ages.

Organizations and the leaders who inhabit them tend to have similar traits. They:

- Tend to distrust people who speak out.
- Label the customers who speak out as troublemakers. If the commentary is from a millennial, then they have even more scrutiny.
- Look at all news as fake news unless they watch, read, or follow it.

This book is designed to help you understand and practice the habits that will change your instinctive responses and seek better options for handling a media crisis.

This is all another way of saying that I have built a business on a phrase:

"What we are is what we repeatedly do."

—Aristotle

CHAPTER 9

HANDLING CRITICISM

HOW TO HANDLE ONLINE CRITICISM

Almost every major brand will face criticism at one time or another. How you handle it will demonstrate a lot about who you are as a company and will either solidify positive relationships with your customers or create an ill will, resulting in losing their business.

In today's world, you're likely to receive customer complaints and criticism online. The key to responding is to avoid deflecting. Instead, connect, and then correct. Here are some examples:

1. Avoid deflection: "I understand what a surprise it must have been to discover how high your bill was this month."
2. Connecting: "I want to help you. Let me explain the charges."
3. Correcting: "The bill was higher than usual this month because your bill wasn't paid last month, and you accrued a charge on top of the missed payment."

ONLINE STAKEHOLDER ACTIVISM: #WEHATEYOU

From my experience in crisis management, one of the most unsettling experiences for a leader is when a collective group targets an organization or its leaders individually. Today, angry stakeholders are more likely than they used to be to cause a crisis for a brand or organization.

The internet—especially social media—has created a place for customers, members, employees, community groups, and individuals with a shared cause, a place to gather to voice complaints or concerns in a collective forum that can create a powerful groundswell incredibly difficult to recover from. The goal is usually to disrupt some part of an operation by exposing legitimate flaws, mismanagement, or lack of transparency that strikes a chord with other activists. Once the groundswell starts, it's tough to stop its force.

I've seen these groups dismantle many projects, plans, and reputations by using savvy social media users who know how to ignite a movement and then apply pressure to change organizational behaviors.

I've worked with a number of clients who are thrown way off kilter by these groups. Out of the blue, Facebook Groups or hashtags will crop up, signaling an attack. Organizations may not even have social media accounts to respond with. If I had to pick one of the biggest vulnerabilities for organizations under attack, it's not having a battlefield to fight on or the weapons to fight back—no Facebook page or social media manager. That is a huge liability. However, indestructibility can be achieved when you know you are being outflanked. The key is to recognize what is happening and adjust accordingly.

This strategy was deployed by the head of the CEO of the National Horsemen's Benevolent and Protective Association. The name of the association may not ring a bell, but the crisis likely will.

The horse racing industry was under siege when it was extensively reported that at least forty-nine equine deaths occurred at the Santa Anita racetrack between July 2018 and June 2019. The vast majority of the deaths were due to breakdown while training or in the midst of a race. Naturally, the horse racing industry was heading well down the stretch for a major crisis. In many cases when a brand hits a snag, the event (or in this case, a series of events) raises the level of scrutiny across the entire industry. Every racetrack and horse racing-affiliated organization or business was at risk of being targeted online. The horse racing industry had to contend with one of the biggest activist groups—PETA, People for the Ethical Treatment of Animals.

From animal actors to exotic animals as pets (they're looking at you, #TigerKing), PETA knows how to grab attention with click-worthy headlines ("The Horseracing Industry: Drugs, Deception and Death") and socially savvy videos. With a number of mainstream media stories airing on network television and printed in national newspapers, the Santa Anita blowback was picking up a lot of steam and to add insult to the horse injuries, a bill—the Horseracing Integrity Act (HR 1754) was being reintroduced in the House to ban the use of all race-day medications. The horse racing industry was in trouble and PETA was leading the charge.

However, Eric Hamelback, the CEO of the National Horsemen's Benevolent and Protective Association (NHBPA) was not going to back down.

Indestructibility in the Threat of Extreme Activism

Hamelback's job was to stop the passage of the bill and attempt to temper the horrendous public opinion being lobbed at the industry. Not an easy task when, as an association, you do not have significant monetary and human resources to tap into to help.

Hamelback used tactics from the Indestructible playbook to stop the bill from passing—and to ensure a win, place or show for his organization's quest for redemption from the public's opinion of the horse racing industry.

Indestructible Playbook for Horse Racing

1. *Identify Liabilities:* Hamelback knew he did not have a large budget or staff to draft and manage a crisis communication plan. There was limited social media and online communication channels to compete against PETA and viral negative news stories.

2. *Identify Strengths:* As a CEO who was passionate about the care of thoroughbred horses, Hamelback knew he could act as an effective spokesperson for his association. He was as comfortable speaking in front of a room as he was to reporters and smart enough to know when to ask for help when he needed it.

3. *Decide and Act:* Hamelback knew he was not in this fight alone. He asked his board for additional funds to hire outside crisis management expertise, especially against online activists. (Sidenote: The crisis management expert he hired was me.)

4. *Speak to Internal Stakeholders First:* Before the public knew the NHBPA's response to the Santa Anita breakdowns, the members of the association were informed of the external communication efforts.

5. *Define Goals and Objectives:* The National Horsemen's Benevolent and Protective Association wanted to be the governing body that encouraged the highest standards of horsemanship to improve the care, health and safety of the horse. The objective was to stop passage of the bill and turn public opinion of horse racing back in their favor.

6. *Identify Key Media:* Hamelback wasn't afraid to call reporters from national newspapers who were clearly writing stories that put his industry in a negative light. He was prepared for every interview with talking points and vetted quotes.

7. *Identify Key Public Audiences:* The competition was neck and neck between public opinion and politics. Hamelback needed to quell the anti-horse racing movement happening in the press and with the negative momentum from online activists while fighting for his industry on Capitol Hill.

8. *Create Key Messages:* These are the core messages that must be conveyed during a crisis. They are clear and concise statements that are repeated frequently at every opportunity. One critical key message used in this campaign was addressing the therapeutic medications, in particular, Lasix, used to combat bleeding that critics of the industry were stating as a contributory factor to the breakdown in thoroughbreds. Hamelback fiercely defended the people who care for the thoroughbreds and reiterated the horses were treated with the highest degree of care.

As for Lasix, he described the use as a medication that was akin to an athlete taking an analgesic before a race. However, he stressed the industry must do more to ensure that each horse everywhere in the United States, is given the attention and protection they deserve. The key message: This is a leader who cares deeply about Thoroughbred racehorses.

9. *Make a Statement:* The first strategy deployed when the crisis was starting to bear down was to make a statement written in the first person. (This statement should be one of the first external communication components to go public.)

10. *Make It Personal:* As stated, one of Hamelback's key messages was unwavering concern for horses. "I believe what I believe because I am passionate about my love for horses," Hamelback told me. Placed in the last paragraphs of his official statement was insight into Hamelback's mindset as a leader—in other words, his noble cause.

11. *Let People See You:* Added to the end of the statement was a photo of Hamelback with his horse. People will hate you less if they see you love something other than yourself.

12. *Go Social:* The statement was sent by email, posted to the NHBPA website, and linked on all their social media platforms.

13. *Invest in Multimedia:* Video is one of the most powerful communication tools to use in a crisis. The more watch time by the public from longer videos increases the chances of your crisis recovery. The NHBPA hired a talented producer, five-time Sports Emmy winner Stuart Kirshenbaum, to film a video of Hamelback at the Thoroughbred Training Center in Lexington, Kentucky. The objective of the video was to now show Hamelback's care and concern for horses and his passion for the industry in a medium that can live in a website and be shared to social media.

14. *Find Additional Stakeholders:* Hamelback spoke to sympathetic reporters and tapped other industry stakeholders to shed light on the caring side of the industry. The NHBPA regularly shared videos of veterinarians caring for horses as well as showing the economic impact to states with racetracks.

The crisis communication plan did not come without taking a toll. Hamelback told me it was emotionally upsetting for him at times to keep fighting his fight, but it was his conviction and maybe arrogance that kept him going because he felt like he was on the right side of the issue. And those animal rights extremists? Hamelback felt like they were not in a position to judge his industry. He was going to fight for what he believed was right.

And the plan? It worked. Yes, the news stories about horse break-downs at racetracks kept getting published, and new stories popped up from the well-worn negativity in the industry. On March 9, 2020, *The New York Times* published a story with a headline that had nothing to do with Hamelback's work, other than to tie the National HBPA back into a crisis by nothing more than an association: "More Than Two Dozen Charged in Horse Racing Doping Scheme."

Hamelback wrote a response statement that he posted to the NHBPA website and shared on their social media accounts. All he could do is hope the story went away.

By March 10, 2020, it did. Posted in *The New York Times*, "U.S. Cases of Coronavirus Surpass 1,000; British Health Minister Is Infected."

A truism in crisis is there is always another one right around the bend.

The key to successful crisis communication management is facing issues head-on with truth and candor. Tell stakeholders what you know, what you believe is correct, and what you will and will not change. Ethical engagement in a time of crisis in the social era can resolve issues naturally if stakeholders sense they are getting most of the story from a trusted spokesperson who is comfortable using the social networks.

CHAPTER 10

THE INDESTRUCTIBLE PLAYBOOK

The Bleeding Edge Communication Guide and Crisis-Response Strategies for Navigating the Culture of Cancellation

BUILD INDESTRUCTIBILITY THROUGH THOUGHT LEADERSHIP

I don't love the term "thought leadership"—I think it's overused—but it conveys the idea better than any other turn of phrase, so for now it stays. The concept is important: leaders should aim at becoming an authority in their specialized fields. This doesn't only apply to entrepreneurs or authors who come up with the next big idea. People who work in organizations can take on thought leadership as a way to bolster their reputation.

The primary goal for most business leaders is to succeed at the goal the company or the board of directors sets out for them. Usually, the bottom line is about the money coming in the door and how it's managed. As an indestructible leader, your goal is to be comfortable in attaching your name to that success. If there is comfort in talking about the admirable work of the business and the top person's role in its success, then a leader should take it.

The one reservation I hear about a leader touting their success or tooting their own horn is pride. I recently heard these three statements made by CEOs of businesses I'm working with:

1. "I don't want to make it about me."
2. "The board of trustees will think I'm bragging."
3. "I was raised Catholic, which meant I was told not to talk about myself in that way." (I told him for what it's worth, I have sixteen years of Catholic School behind me and I never remember hearing that edict.)

Don't look at thought leadership as bragging. It's sharing your knowledge and your experience to *help* people, especially those in the same industry or circumstance.

Here's the indestructible part—thought leadership can be used to boost, secure, or rebuild your reputation when you need it and when you don't.

Here's how to become a thought leader:

1. Find your hook. Why does your point of view matter over someone else in the same industry? There are likely many leaders who inhabit the same space as you, but you have the guts to show the world why you're different.
2. Figure out who your key audience is, then create content around their wants, needs, and fears.
3. Identify the outlets where you can reach your key audience when the time is right. If your industry is in the news, then its leader needs to be as well.

Five Ways to Solidify Your Role as a Thought Leader

1. **Social Media**. It's time. You've put it off long enough. Every organization—consumer, for-profit, cooperative, non-profit, business-to-business—needs to have a social media presence. If the brand has one, then so should its leadership. Now, remember—"presence" does not mean everywhere, it just means somewhere. Every twenty-first-century leader needs to hang

their hat on a social network. Thought leaders use one or more to publish ideas and their expertise in their field.

2. **Blog**. It seemed like the first website of every company or organization had a blog, and then once it was decided they were too difficult to maintain, they were tossed aside or left for dead. While some say podcasts are the new blogs, that doesn't mean blogs are digitally antiquated. I still believe in the power of blogging. It helps with SEO and offers a place for employees and leaders of an organization to create content to share on social channels. Consumers may not be clicking onto your blog in droves, but a dedicated blog does give your organization a place to share their news and commentary. And who better to share it than the leader of the company?

3. **Podcast**. My favorite medium for creating or sharing thought leadership is the podcast. Whether your organization publishes an internal podcast for employees or shares a public show with the universe, podcasting is quick and a—let's face it—cool way to get a leader's opinions to the masses.

4. **Contributed Content**. Publications, reporters, and podcasts want to hear from thought leaders. Look for bylines and soundbites to push your authority outside of your typical audience. Write a guest column, be interviewed for a book—or even better, write the book yourself.

5. **Press Hits**. Many organizations have communication staffs for creating and pushing content out onto social media, but how are they pushing stories to the media? In my experience, media pitching has been on the decline since social media took hold. The companies that do expect their communications staff to pitch often leave it in the hands of junior staffers who don't have much experience working with journalists. Use media relations to pitch your business and also your leadership. Have your public relations staff pitch you as a spokesperson for feature articles or in the trades. News jacking (finding a hook related to a trending news story) is perfect for the viral environment because journalists are scouring for spokespeople. Once you are on a journalist's radar, they know they can come back to you again in the future.

BUILD INDESTRUCTIBILITY THROUGH SOCIAL MEDIA

Social media is the key to making yourself an indestructible leader who is unafraid of being transparent on social media and during media interviews, who manages criticism skillfully and stays in front of the public eye.

Use the following list as a guide to what you must, should, and could have in order to be a leader in your industry online.

MUST-HAVES FOR LEADERS

Robust Personal LinkedIn Profile

LinkedIn is a must-have for anyone in a professional setting—whether you're a business owner or an executive. It's also the easiest place to start getting to know social media better without the reputational risk. Make sure your profile is filled out completely, including a professional photo, your background, your current position, and a professionally written bio.

Business LinkedIn Page

Similarly, your organization should have a LinkedIn page so you and your team can link to it in your own profile. The business LinkedIn page is a place where you can position your organization as a leader in the industry and be fully transparent about its mission and values. Plus, it allows people to view an actual logo and not a nondescript gray building.

SHOULD-HAVES FOR LEADERS

Active Twitter Account

Twitter isn't solely for silly opinions and political positioning and pandering. When used well, it's a leadership platform where you can stay abreast of top news in your industry and be an active part of the conversation. Understand and utilize hashtags. The handy "pound sign" offers a way to group and categorize tweets. Place a "#" in front of a person's name, word, or trending news story on Twitter and you are given the choice of the top or latest tweets with the same hashtag. The hashtags help find relevant tweets immediately rather than having to scroll through all the Twitter universe.

LinkedIn Engagement

Having a presence on LinkedIn is a must but engaging on the site takes additional effort. LinkedIn is the perfect place to engage and network with others in your industry. Like Twitter, it's a source of news and information and has a useful recruitment tool for your organization. Explore posts by others in your industry. Add your own posts. Comment on and share relevant posts.

COULD-HAVES FOR LEADERS

YouTube Channel & Social Media Video

Nothing says transparency like a leader talking directly to the camera. Videos can be one-off talks about the latest news in your organization, planned events each week or month, or fun anecdotes about the industry. Whatever way you plan the videos, make sure they're well-lit, the sound is high quality, and that you're open to feedback from your team, the public, and the media.

A Podcast

Nothing says "I'm a thought leader" more than investing your time and tech budget into creating a podcast to promote your mission. People are already spending a lot of time listening to podcasts, and the amount keeps growing. Talk about news, stories, principles, events, or updates related to your field.

CONCLUSION

What a true leader looks like and what they represent transcends time. It comes down to power, hard work, direction, inspiration, and a mission. Anyone can succeed as a leader if they want to ascend for the right reasons. Of course, all leaders want to succeed and command respect, but with the increase in technology and the subsequent shift in business and culture, there has also been a subsequent shift in what people expect from a leader.

Not long ago, leaders at the top of the rung were allowed to squirrel themselves away to run the company. It was up to the communications staff to deliver messages to the stakeholders. Public relations professionals were there to craft and deliver messaging to the press to garner the best news coverage possible while speaking on behalf of the leadership. Reporters would want to get the furthest up the rung to get to the bottom of the story, but it was generally accepted the person at the top didn't need to provide any response. That was up to the communication staff.

The intimate relationship between the press and the press shop was blown open. The public now has more access to information than ever before, and their thirst for information never ends. With so much information available on the internet, people are more accustomed to finding information at their fingertips.

Because the public has come to expect immediate information, they often go to any source to get it. When someone can type any query into a search engine and receive results in moments, they're far less willing to wait for information or be patient with anyone withholding information. When the internet is sluggish, they get frustrated. The same applies to a company with poor customer service or offers a bad user experience online. If the contact information for company representatives are not listed on the website, the public starts to suspect that they do not want the public to know who works there or that the company is preventing them from contacting anyone.

Often when I work with a company, I end up having this conversation.

Me: "Why don't you have the names of your employees on the website? Or your board of directors? Your CEO?"

The response: "We don't want just anyone to reach out to us."

Me: "What if they came to your lobby and asked to speak with an employee? Would you tell your customer they have no right to speak to an employee or representative from the company?"

Of course, not all employees of a company are front-facing and deal directly with the customer. There are many legitimate reasons for not listing every employee on a website, but there's a big difference between not wanting to list names for privacy's sake and not wanting to list a name because it's no one's business. But if you think it's no one's business, do you have a problem with an employee listing their employment on LinkedIn or their personal Facebook page? The answer is usually no.

So many of the objections that I hear from people in business—usually leaders—stems from this need for privacy. "What we do to run this business is nobody's business." But look at how much money is spent on advertising, marketing, and sales—and you don't want anybody to know anything about your business? The danger of this privacy mindset is that it limits one of the most powerful aspects of connecting with the customers: revealing a behind-the-scenes look of your business.

That's when it's time to reflect on the reflexive move to withhold information from the public. Almost always, that reflex is motivated by one thing: fear.

Fear of being found out.

Fear of the public knowing too much.

Fear of someone catching you inadvertently doing something wrong.

Fear of being caught deliberately doing something wrong.

Fear of being harassed.

Fear of the public forming the wrong opinion of you.

And that list goes on and on. This idea of fear is so prevalent in online media nowadays. When I started to process the idea of fear and vulnerability, I kept reflecting on the well-known and often-misunderstood quote from Franklin Delano Roosevelt.

I've often heard the recording of FDR giving his inaugural address to the American public in 1933 during the financial crisis of the time. But I never fully grasped its meaning in its correct context. I only truly got the meaning when I started to notice the prevalence of fear in so many of my executive clients. Then Roosevelt's words now made all the sense in the world to me.

The entire line said by Roosevelt was, "So, first of all, let me assert my firm belief that **the only thing we have to fear is fear itself**—nameless, unreasoning, unjustified terror which paralyzes needed efforts to convert retreat into advance."

This statement is even more relevant in the context of advancing into technology and digital media instead of retreating into fear of financial ruin.

When a leader fears the introduction of digital or social media into the business, when that fear becomes "nameless, unreasoning, unjustified terror," that fear "paralyzes needed efforts to convert retreat into advance," —into indestructible leadership.

"I don't want a company Facebook page."

Well, over one billion people use Facebook. It stands a good chance that your customer is one of those billion Facebook users. To refrain from using one of the most powerful communication channels in the world is a fear that frankly can't be named.

"I don't want to put financial information about the company on our website for our customers to see. Even if they can find the same information on another website, I don't want to have to include it on the company website just because someone wants us to."

To force your customer to go through extra efforts to retrieve information about your business from another website is unreasonable.

"I do not want to speak with the press. Everything they report is fake news anyway. They will edit the videotape how they want and misconstrue my meaning."

The terror of a bad press interview is palpable, but refusing to participate in a news story because you believe every reporter is out to get you is unjustified. True, there are reporters who report with an agenda. And yes, there are news organizations that distort the truth. But those instances are far fewer than most would believe. Reporters who follow the ethics of journalism are only out to get a story.

These are the types of fears that are only making it worse.

Falling victim to fear means you are preventing yourself from telling your side of the story to the press and, most important, your customers—the customers who keep you in business.

There is a common saying in the public relations industry: if you fail to tell your story, someone will always tell it for you. And they always do. And when they do it, it may not be pretty.

From my experience, I think one of the best ways to build a relationship with a customer is to build trust between you. By letting the customer know that you want to bring them in on the inside, they will be open to your mission and values and how you do business. And if there is a part of your business that does not sit well with the customer, or when things go sideways, you can rely on all that goodwill and trust to keep that customer on your side.

Leading by truth makes you trustworthy. Leading by fear makes your customer lose trust in you and you lose credibility. What does it mean to be trustworthy? It means being open, honest, and genuine when things are good, but especially, when they aren't.

Some people call reality television the scourge of artistic entertainment, but if that's the case, why is it so popular? After decades of highly produced television with laugh tracks and studio audiences, viewers started to grow a little tired of the false front portrayed on television. Years of iconic characters from *Murphy Brown, M.A.S.H., Roseanne, Married with Children*, and *E.R.* brought huge ratings for networks catering to particular demographics. But the iconic leads in these programs turned out in many cases to be different in real life. Bill Cosby, in the heyday of the *Cosby Show*, was the most popular father on television. A few decades later everyone would see the truly dark side of Dr. Huxtable.

In hindsight, it isn't surprising that people started to lose interest in scripted television when cable news started to grow in popularity in the early '90s. People are now wired to expect unscripted television, and nothing gets more real than news. When the money started to come in, it was likely then that networks saw the riches in reality television. When MTV introduced *The Real World* in 1992, a new format was born.[14] Yes, people wanted their MTV, but they also wanted real-time footage of real-life situations from people who looked a lot like them. The next generation of television viewers loved the rawness of people letting it all out, and just like that, a new reality was born.

Fast forward decades later and reality television is now the dominate format for viewers. The low cost of production combined with the unpredictability of episodes created a format that was perfectly suited for an age of personal online media. There is a reason why Netflix is a $1.8 billion-dollar company—and it's not only from the pandemic. People love reality media.

If there were ever a true secret sauce to build a trust connection with your customer, it would be to manage your role in the business like a reality show. Be the executive producer of your own program. You are in charge of the script and the production. You decide what the public sees and why. Follow the success of reality television to ascertain exactly what the public is craving at the moment.

Now, I'm not going to suggest you flip a table over or film your encounter with other Housewives of New Jersey or Atlanta, but the appeal is letting people into the day-to-day of running a business. What is it like to run the business of you?

Most business websites have a mission statement on their website. Check the "About Us" tab on the website to find all the dry content about what a company does and who they market to. Look under the "News" section of a website to see the latest news releases and newsletter about the information that is safe for viewing.

But show me the company that has a section dedicated to its leadership and to the mission and value statements. That's a company that will get people on its side quickly when they need to. Let me watch a video of the CEO talking to the camera. Show me scenes away from behind the desk. Show me interaction with the customers and with the public. Let me in, and I will let you sell to me.

---

14. Sidenote: When *The Real World* aired, I was working at a Twin Cities rock station 93x. I thought I could parlay the gig into a spot on *The Real World*. Who wouldn't want to cast a girl living in St. Paul, Minnesota, who worked at an alternative/hard rock station who played softball and broomball on a co-ed bar league? It turns out, the producers at MTV, that's who.

It is as simple as that.

Past . . . here's the secret: the more information you designate public, the more your detractors or customers angling for a disagreement will lay off you. It is the opposite of how it feels, I know. Time and time again, I see and hear the arguments for why an organization does not share information to its public. For instance, when I work with cooperatives, I deal with a group of people working or representing an organization owned by its members. The cooperative business model is built around the Seven Cooperative Principles, the Rochdale model.

- **Voluntary** and Open Membership
- Democratic Member **Control**
- Members' Economic Participation
- Autonomy and Independence
- **Education**, Training, and Information
- Cooperation among Cooperatives
- Concern for Community

Yet this is what I hear from cooperatives:

- "We would never tell our members of the co-op how much the CEO earns annually. That is none of their business."
- "We would never tell the members how much a director or trustee is compensated for their role on the board. They would take that number and turn it against us."
- "We would never release the salary of our employees' earning over $100,000 because our members and the press would turn it against us."

While cooperatives often claim to be all about the democratic process—"Serving the business means serving the member"—and sound like organizations that should not struggle with the concepts of truth and transparency, they do in many cases. I'm talking about credit unions, utilities, worker cooperatives, purchasing cooperatives. Cabot Cheese, Ace Hardware, Welch's Grape Juice—you get the idea.

I don't hear this language from only one co-op; I hear it over, and over again, from the general manager to the head of billing. The reluctance is almost ingrained in them. The circumstances may change a bit, the lexicon they use may be different, but the feelings are all the same.

"That information is not the members' business." But since the mission of a co-op is to serve the member, it is a weak argument. "But what do we do if the information gets out and is out of our control?" That's the fear talking.

I have made a business out of helping people get comfortable communicating online and not let the fear of public backlash get to them. Humans are hard-wired to get nervous putting themselves "out there." It's understandable. However, by adopting a Jiu jitsu mentality of using your weakness to overcome fear, you can not only protect but build your reputation by sharing a little more information about yourself that you normally would with the public. Leading by authenticity shows the public your passion and—this is important—your values.

If you run a business in transportation, maybe your passion is the safety and security of your customer.

If you have a service-based business, maybe it's providing the customer with the best service possible.

If you are a business owner who teaches people how to knit, your passion could be showing people how to excel at knitting.

If you are a book coach, your passion could be helping people write their first book.

A passion statement sounds a lot like a mission statement, but in many cases it's a lot more colorful. That is why I encourage leaders to revisit their companies' mission statements. If it's dry and formulaic, then you may end up treating your customer with the same mechanical feeling.

But if a mission statement has passion woven into the wording, it's a surefire way to get the customer excited about you. Let that passion be contagious. People are more likely to trust someone who has an "all-in" vibe to them about the work they do.

PARTING THOUGHTS

If you've made it this far in the book, then now, my friend, it is no longer some generic professional development book you toss aside. (If you plan to stash it away anyway, I'd prefer you place it on a shelf. The colorful spine is perfect for Zoom calls.) Whether the book stays or not—I hope the premise stays with you longer. This playbook contains the secret for combating personal or professional attacks that find their way online and run the risk of destroying your reputation.

From rapid response to thoughtful messaging, you have the PR artillery and ammunition to survive any surprise or planned attack against you or your brand. You may not win every skirmish, but you will win the war and your reputation will live to see another day.

Remember, your foremost weapon in your arsenal is intelligence. Admit to yourself what you do not understand, and then seek to learn it. It's understandable to not have the time or desire to learn every bell and whistle of social media. Many people don't like being taught anything once they leave school. Even Winston Churchill said, "Personally I'm always ready to learn, although I do not always like being taught."

Fair enough.

However, if you learn anything from this book, learn the importance of having a mindset for accepting change. Don't resist it. Yes, there are plenty of people who do not want to bother with online conversations or change their use of technology. I get it. It's easier to stay safe with what you know and what you feel comfortable using. But complacency can get pretty lonely here.

To effectively communicate in this era of digital media, you need to find a comfort level with technology that meets you where you are at the moment but offers plenty of space to grow along with your expertise. Be comfortable with your own pace and not intimidated when it feels like other people are speaking a different language. Be open to sharing your principles on an open platform and steadfast enough when someone tells you they disagree. Let your passion guide you when you create content to share with the world, but never forget to be fearlessly committed to embracing the idea that your thoughts, opinions, and advice matter to someone else.

Remember: When you make a mistake—admit it. Explain what happened, and what will change so it doesn't happen again.

Do all of this, and you will become . . .

Indestructible.

A NOTE FROM MOLLY

Every crisis will do one of two things to a reputation: Build it or burn it. That's where I come in.

I help people and organizations build their reputations even if it is in the process of being destroyed. I do that by creating frameworks for people to use to make their public relations response indestructible.

With a mission of helping people gain confidence in their external communications in a digital age where people are afraid to say the wrong thing at the wrong time and in the wrong place, I provide relief and direction for how to get it right.

Do I have the final word on how to do just that?

No. The online and social media landscape changes so often that no one, in my opinion, has solid footing—the ground is constantly shifting. Understanding every nuance of every media channel and social networking platform is impossible.

But I do have a passion for this and a number of tricks that seem to help people—especially leaders and communicators—build their confidence to create an online brand and hit the ground running.

If they run into a crisis, I have an Indestructible PR™ framework that help them survive it. Every time.

If they are run over by a crisis, I have an indestructible PR crisis response that helps them recover quickly and even come back better than ever before.

The key to conquering social media is knowing you never will. But you can find your safe space where you feel confident and understand how to use the medium.

That's where you build your brand.

That where you share helpful content to help people solve their problems.

That's where you will fight when a crisis hits.

The secret to PR indestructibility is knowing what your strengths and weaknesses are before your opponents do.

Always be aware of the threats to your name and always look for the opportunities for sharing your strengths when it comes to helping people.

Use it for your professional life.

Use it for your life.

THIS BOOK WAS MEANT FOR THIS YEAR

The year 2020 was challenging for me. Recognizing the COVID-19 pandemic made life difficult for everyone, but when running a company that relied on public speaking, it seemed as if the ground under me was always shaking and never stable.

Could I support a public speaking and media training business, not to mention a family, when nobody was meeting in person? The answer was not really.

One by one, the bookings were cancelled. By the second week of April, 90 percent of my 2020 bookings were gone and I had no idea when the work would return.

To add to the instability: I was writing a book about managing a crisis while trying to survive one.

All in all—a perfect time for writing a book.

Not really.

As with every crisis, there's always more.

Writing a book with four kids who have the typical demands of teenagers makes it very hard. Trying to write it while their world was turned sideways by a pandemic was extraordinarily hard.

Pulling a book together while my 20-year marriage was coming apart at the seams?

Stress: unyielding.

Lessons: abound.

Well, it's good that the book was about how to deal with a crisis, because it turns out I was pretty good at it.

It would have been so easy to put this book off to another year. But 2020 was the year that crisis and communication were connected in a way that I had never seen before in my over 25 years in public relations, communications and journalism.

It recognized the common thread of crisis response to human response. Experiencing this critical year, both professionally and personally, taught me that managing a crisis was as much about understanding the mechanics behind why a crisis occurred as it was about understanding the mindset of the people who caused it.

In a year when so much was upended by a deadly pandemic, there was always the need for open and honest communication.

No one could have prepared themselves for this extraordinary crisis. It is the definition of an unknown unknown that no one could predict.

It was my time whether I knew it or not. I was made not only to survive a pandemic, but also to thrive.

On March 2, 2020, I was in New Orleans speaking at the Annual Meeting for the National Rural Electric Cooperative Association. I felt like I was in the minority of people concerned about the coronavirus. I had already stepped up my handwashing and didn't greet people by shaking hands. That was why few people were concerned I lost my voice the night before somewhere between dinner and the piano bar at 2:00 a.m.

But I didn't lose it on stage because I was speaking on a panel about my favorite topic: online reputation management and crisis communications. *(I feel a person has found their calling in life when they find a topic that is as exciting to talk about with friends over drinks as it would be on stage.)*

Had I known then what I know now, I would have told everyone from the stage that day only one thing about communications: Invest in it now for your organization because it will be your most important department in a matter of days.

After New Orleans, it was a one-day stop in Fargo, North Dakota, to serve as a keynote speaker at a meeting for an insurance company. *Aside*: Everyone in North Dakota is nice. The hosts left me the local delicacy Chippers (chocolate-covered chips) in my hotel room and I was in love. Not normal for a girl born and raised in Minnesota.

One unforgettable line I heard from one of my hosts about the coronavirus that was starting to spread was "It will blow over in a few weeks." I had already ordered facemasks from Amazon at that point, so I was making a mental note that North Dakota might get hit hard.

By the time I landed at Minneapolis-St. Paul Airport the next day, almost everyone in the airport was wearing masks. On the connecting flight to Boston, I was already thinking about the impact of the pandemic on life and on work.

Sitting on the smooth flight back home that night, I knew I was in for a ride. Who knew it would last so long?

At the time of this writing, the coronavirus is still very much a part of everyday life but so much of our everyday communications has changed in the past year.

THE NEW NOW

I am a forever optimist. I spent the pandemic year looking for all the silver linings in my work:

New technology
New terminology
New way of doing business
New communication channels
Newfound confidence in all of the above.

MOLLY DEFINED

I found strength in my struggles by helping people overcome theirs in online communications. I do it for myself.

Proving German philosopher Friedrich Nietzsche's adage that "what does not kill me makes me stronger," I wrote a book. And I wrote during the most difficult time of my life.

If 2020 taught me anything, it's that living authentically with a value system buttressed with honesty, determination, hard work, good ethics, and treating others with respect and decency will make you indestructible.

MY APPRECIATION

Only my name is on the book as the author, but so many people have helped me and inspired me to get to where I am today.

To all the people who have attended my talks, participated in workshops, listened to my podcasts, or interacted with me on social media, thank you for inspiring me to keep learning and to keep sharing.

To the people who make up the hamlets of a life from moving from St. Paul to Boston then Washington, DC, and back to New England, my happiness and strength comes from knowing (and likely laughing) with you.

Thank you to all my teammates over the last five years. Your supreme talents have helped me get where I am now. Particular thanks to my producer Scott "Minnesota" Wild for giving me the puck. Your abilities are remarkable.

To my publishers, Azul Terronez and Steve Vannoy, you guys get it and I'm so grateful that you do.

To my team who helped me survive and thrive—especially Scott W. the W stands for my Right Wing)—your talent on the ice is remarkable. Thanks for giving me the puck.

To all my friends who connected with me by phone, text or email at any time in the 2020 pandemic year, you're my gang. Thank you for being there for me. Kelley and My Vineyard Crew, your texts and friendships humored and sustained me in the day-to-day. Thank you. I hold you all near and dear.

To my family, you're like my Carbone's gluten-free pizza. Wish I could see it a lot more but grateful to know there is something to look forward to when I can go back to Minnesota. Seriously, your steadfast support is everything. Mike, thank you for your podcast reviews. It's like having George Martin giving me feedback in Abbey Road Studios.

To my home team, Rory, Kathleen, Conor, and Quinn, along with our team mascot, Finbar—all day, every day is for you. I love you.

All of you make me feel indestructible.

ABOUT THE AUTHOR

Molly McPherson, M.S., APR is a nationally recognized expert on public relations and crisis response in the digtial age. She combines her knowledge of current communication practices with years of media and crisis management experience to help organizations manage issues—from emerging to a crisis—to ensure organizations surface with their reputation intact. Molly is an authority on helping communicators create the right message and the right time and deliver it in the right place.

Host of the podcast "Confident Communications with Molly McPherson," she frequently speaks about communication trends, crisis communications, public relations, and social media crisis response to executives and organizations. Through her experience in FEMA's Office of External Affairs during post-Hurricane Katrina efforts and as Director of Communications for the Cruise Line International Association in Arlington, Virginia, Molly created a proven public relations framework for responding to a public backlash both online and in the press.

She is firmly grounded in the belief that communicating trust and transparency both online and off is key to an organization's success in the digital age.

Molly is always running. In a race, on deadline, to her kids' hockey or soccer games, or with her Portuguese water dog, Finbar—who come to think of it—prefers a long walk anyway. No one likes to run on a beach anyway.

CPSIA information can be obtained
at www.ICGtesting.com
Printed in the USA
LVHW090004240421
685378LV00029BA/671/J